# IS THERE ANYBODY OUT THERE?

# IS THERE ANYBODY OUT THERE?

### Mez McConnell

#### Edited by Irene Howat

CHRISTIAN FOCUS

© Mez McConnell

ISBN 1-84550-205-1
ISBN 978-1-84550-205-8

10 9 8 7 6 5 4 3 2 1

Published in 2006
by
Christian Focus Publications Ltd.,
Geanies House, Fearn, Tain,
Ross-shire, IV20 1TW, Great Britain
www.christianfocus.com

Cover design by Moose77.com

Printed and bound by Nørhaven Paperback A/S, Denmark

# IS THERE ANYBODY OUT THERE?

## Mez McConnell

## Contents

# ACKNOWLEDGMENTS

There are so many people to thank that it is impossible to know where to start. These are in no direct order.

Matthew Stinson, wherever you are, thanks for taking the time to sit down with an angry young man and then visit him in prison. You will always be the guy who introduced me to Christ. Dave Pierce, what can I say? It began with a prayer in a parked car. Much love to you, more than you even know. Mark Trafford, for the quality discipleship which sustained me more than you will ever realise. Ben Pike and family (Rachel, Thomas, Joshua, James and Levi), who knew where a visit to Armley Prison would lead us? Thanks for all the support over the years, and for the prayers, counsel, words of wisdom and the 'pull yourself together' talks.

Thank you, Steff and Paula James. PJ, you were my first Christian pen pal in Armley, and Steff, the first 'ordinary bloke' who stuck by me in the early years. Thanks for putting up with me even when I was being a pain. Mr and Mrs F. - my first pastor and a true man of God. I learned so much from you, in particular a deep and reverent regard for the Bible. You will always be special to me. Joan and Bernard Maquire, I have too much to thank you for and not enough space in which to do it. You are not directly found within the pages of this book but you both know what a huge part you played in my spiritual life in the early years. You even put up with the 'hatch banging'! Thank you.

Molly and Rod Frampton, thank you for sticking with us when others turned their backs. You are a priceless couple who will always have our undying love and devotion. Chris and Christina Hands, for your friendship and for keeping me sane during the mad college years. Steve and Fiona Utley, for our enduring friendship since the college years and for the introduction to Top Wok. Thank you, Jason and Vicki White for your encouragement and support.

There are so many more who deserve my thanks: Len & Liz Doyle, Stuart D, Jez Dearing, Pete Mountford, Gareth and Sue Illey, Gareth and Corina Morgan, to name a few. And special thanks are due to all at Swindon Evangelical Church (BIAC), South Birmingham Evangelical Church, North Swindon Baptist Church and to all of the young people from my first church down south. Thank you to everyone who has sustained and supported us financially over the years and to all at UFM for your continuous support.

Thank you, Peter and Joy Hillier, Emma and Lee, for all the encouraging phone calls and webcams. Peter Milsom, you're a really good bloke to put up with my occasional rants and raves. George and Andrea White, words can't even begin to describe how much your friendship means to me and to us as a family. Thanks for all the crazy notes and the 'free minutes' and the visits to see our work.

Thanks, Irene for your hard work in editing away my rough edges but allowing me to keep some of them.

And my special thanks goes to my wife Miriam and my little girls Keziah and Lydia. All I have is love for you all. Always.

To any and all I may not have mentioned but who have walked with me a while on my pilgrimage thus far, thank you.

Finally, this book is dedicated to Rev. Dr. Steven Dray who believed in me when everybody doubted.

Mez McConnell

# FOREWORD

Every story must have a beginning. Every story has to start somewhere. I suppose that's one of the unbreakable rules of storytelling. Beginnings are important. We look back on them through the medium of our memories and what we find there often defines who we are today. Our beginnings don't have to define us, of course, but the reality is that they affect us more than many of us care to admit. They can drive us onward and upward or they can drive us onward and downward. In either case they usually do drive us.

We're all writing stories, every single one of us, whether we realise it or not. We're all banking memories, adding to them, storing them up for a day when we can cash them in, when we can sit back and wallow in them, remembering the things we've done, the places we've gone, the people we've met and the experiences we've had. That's not true for everyone, of course. Some of us, many of us, are running away from our memories and trying to forget our experiences. Some of us, many of us, are trying hard to erase our past experiences by how we live in the present. We try to smother them with drink, drugs, sex or work. But that's an exercise in futility. All we are really doing is extending our nightmares and adding more experiences that, sooner or later, we will need to work harder to forget.

We all want to leave our mark on the world. We all want our story to be heard, to be told by strangers. We want to be remembered, immortalised … somehow. We want it all to have meant something. However meaningless we think it all is, we still want our lives to mean *something, anything*. We want to be heard, to be noticed, accepted and admired.

Who knows our inmost being? Who knows what we really think and what we feel? Who knows our story? Who can see the world as we see it? Who sees through our eyes? We are our own interpreters. We make our own memories. We understand our experiences in our own unique way. No two stories are ever the same. No human story is ever understood universally. We all read it and understand it in our own way. We all take different lessons from it.

Yet there is one story, a cosmic story, that's being written, that has been written, that is constantly being told. We are living in it. We are a microscopic part of it. When understood it gives our own stories meaning. It adds hope to our memories and it supersedes all of our interpretations.

This is my story.

# 1

# MEMORIES

My story starts before I was even born. My parents, who married at a very young age in the Republic of Ireland in the early Seventies, had problems from the outset. My grandfather on my dad's side committed suicide when Dad was a young boy. Apparently he stuck his head in an oven and just turned on the gas. Dad's mother then abandoned him and his young brothers. I think there were four of them. I'm not sure. It's not something I've ever discussed in depth with my father. All I know for sure is that somehow Dad ended up moving from his birthplace in Scotland to Ireland whilst the others were spread out across the world. He never saw two of his brothers again. There's a story right there just waiting to be told. But, sadly, it will be lost by the passage of time because there is nobody around to tell it.

The marriage between my parents appeared to be doomed from the start. Neither has offered a satisfactory explanation. Both remember things from their own perspective; both hold on to their own version of the truth. The reality, I imagine, is somewhere in between. But, for whatever reasons, it was my mother who ran off when I was two years old leaving my three-year-old sister and me with her mother. There's a sort of perverse cosmic parallel there, I suppose.

**Alone**

*I'm at the doctor and he sticks a needle into my arm. I cry and look for mummy. But she isn't there. I am alone.*

*'Where's my mummy?'*

*It's Christmas morning. Where's Mummy? I got some sweets for Christmas and I want to show her. I can't find her.*

Apart from that I don't really have any conscious memory of my mother. There was never any sense of physical loss. One day I woke up and she wasn't there. She was never there again.

*I've got a bright red tractor with some sweets in the back. It's a present for my birthday, I think. Mummy's not here but Daddy is. I peddle into my dad's bedroom and he's lying propped up on his pillow, grinning at me. I give him a sweet and peddle away. I still don't know where Mummy is.*

*I'm sitting on Grandma's settee with my sister. Granddad is hitting my dad. I haven't seen Dad for a long time. Grandma gives me juice and a boiled egg. Dad goes away again. He's always going away. But at least he always comes back. Mummy hasn't come back. He said that Mummy is never coming back.*

I'm told that my sister and I spent a great deal of our early years with my grandparents on my mother's side. If I'm honest I can't remember that either. I want to remember them both with fondness and happiness, but I can't. Sometimes I close my eyes and try to remember what they look like, but I can't. Sometimes I think that it would be nice to have Waltonesque memories, or at least to invent some of my own. I just remember that they were there somewhere in the background. The one thing I do remember about them is that I felt happy and secure when they were around.

I don't even know their names.

*We're driving in the car with my dad. It's late at night and we stop on the motorway. A woman gets in. I've never seen her before. We keep on driving and it starts to rain. Who is she? Is she my mum? Maybe. Daddy is kissing her.*

*Dad's gone. I don't know where. This woman is looking after us. She's not very nice. When she gets angry she hits us. She gets angry a lot.*

*Dad's back. The hitting has stopped. But then he goes away and the hitting starts again.*

*We've come to visit a big house. Dad says we have to stay here for a while. He doesn't say why. There are lots of other children here. I think their dads have left them for a while too. I cry a lot. But nobody hits my sister or me. I sleep in a big room with lots of other boys. The house is so big and has a back garden with a sandpit and a huge tree that we climb when nobody is looking. Dad comes back but then he goes away again.*

*It's my birthday. I'm seven and I have a party at the big house. I've never had a party before. I have cake and everyone sings to me. Where's my dad? I feel alone.*

*I love it in the big house. I have loads of friends and we're allowed out to go to church once a week. We get to see the nuns singing. If we're good on the way there we're allowed to have ice cream on the way back.*

*One day two ladies come to see me. They are very nice and they start to take me out every week. Sometimes we go to their house and they give me treats. Sometimes they take me shopping. Once they took me to the cinema. I wish they could be my mum. But I always have to go back to the big house every week.*

*My dad has come back and we have to leave the big house. I have to leave my friends. I have to leave the two ladies. I feel alone again.*

*We move into a new house. One day men come with the police and throw us on to the street. We have nowhere to live and we have nothing to eat. Sometimes I wonder about my mum. Does she have a house? Does she have things to eat? Does she ever think about me, about my sister? Does she ever feel alone?*

## Across the water

*We're on a boat now. We have to get past soldiers with big guns. They look in our suitcase. They look very angry.*

*We're on our way to England. It's very stormy outside and my plate of egg and chips is sliding about all over the table. Maybe my mum is in England.*

*England is an awful place. We haven't found my mum yet. We move from one cramped, squalid bedsit to another. Finally, we arrive in Yorkshire and move into a house. My dad is away a lot. The hitting starts again.*

*Our house is cold and damp. There's no carpet on the floors or paper on the walls. I have a bed and a blanket and a million bed bugs. They're small and red, and they live in my mattress and in the folds of the curtains. They come out at night. I know they're coming because they smell funny. They crawl on my face, my eyes and my hair. I get used to them.*

*I'm hungry. Dad lost his wages on the horses again. Dad is always in the betting shop. Sometimes SHE sends me down there to get him. Dad looks embarrassed when I go in and he always makes me wait outside for him. I daren't go back without him because if I do, SHE hits me.*

*I'm hungry. There's not enough food this week. There's enough for cigarettes and beer but not for food. Dad disappears again and I'm locked in my room without food. It's worse in the holidays because I have to stay there for days on end. I feel alone.*

*Sometimes I'm sent to the shop for bread and milk and I open the bread up, steal a slice from it, and replace the top. I have to hurry back though, because if I take more than five minutes SHE beats me. If I do it in less SHE beats me. I have to time it just right.*

*I'm so hungry.*

*Sometimes I lie in bed at night and wonder what it would be like not to be hit. In my head I transport myself into the future where I'm big and strong. There is no hitting in my dreams. I can't even remember when the hitting started. I can't remember what it's like not to be hit.*

*Sometimes, if I'm lucky, I just get slapped on the head. Often I'm punched on the back of the head and the kidneys. The punch to the kidneys hurts the most. I try and avoid that if I can. It usually means leaving my head wide open, but anything is better than the kidneys. I try to avoid curling up on the floor because SHE kicks me in the testicles. I don't cry out any more for it doesn't do any good. Sometimes I wonder where my mother is. This is all her fault.*

*It was a sweeping brush handle today. I didn't dry the dishes fast enough. The floor was dirty. The bin was overflowing. I can't remember why I'm being hit anymore. My back hurts.*

*Her friends are around again. They are all drunk in the front room. SHE screams for me. I get out of bed and go to her. SHE flicks lit cigarette butts at my head when SHE's drunk. SHE spits on me. Her friends laugh at me.*

*I'm allowed to go to London for the day with my classmates. I've got egg sandwiches and a whole pound to spend. I buy her a box of Roses for 99p. I don't know why. Sometimes I think that if I'm nice to her then maybe SHE'll be nice to me back. I come home and SHE is in the front room drinking with her friends. SHE's drunk. I give her the chocolates and SHE punches me in the face. All her friends laugh at me. I go to my room and cry. I really am alone. I rock myself to sleep and dream that my mother is going to come and rescue me. She's going to knock on the door one day and take me back to Ireland where nobody gets hit.*

*SHE's drunk again. I can hear her snoring in the bedroom next to mine. Dad is out. I get some paper, screw it up and shove it under the bed. Using her matches I set it on fire. I hope SHE burns. Dad comes back and sees the smoke. He wakes her up. The paper didn't catch properly. Shame. I don't think he realises it was me.*

*It's late at night. They're coming to take me away. I'm going to a children's home. My sister and I are separated. That's never happened before. I wonder if I'll ever see her again. When I get into the building they're having their supper of toast and milk. Everybody's looking at me. Stuff 'em! Toast and milk! You don't get that every day. If I'd known this would happen I would have tried to set her on fire sooner.*

*I've to move to a new school, but I don't have any clothes and I've only got Wellington boots. They take me down to the cellar and show me a room full of clothes and shoes. It's like a big shop. They let me choose what I like. They let me choose! I've got a clean shirt and shiny shoes without holes! My clothes are ironed and everything! How cool is that! I feel on top of the world. I wonder what they would have given me for killing her.*

*I like my new school and I'm a shepherd in the school nativity play. My friends from the home come and see me. Everyone is clapping and cheering for me. Nobody has ever done that before.*

*It's snowing. One of the older girls helps me build an igloo in the back garden. I'm happy again. There's no hitting or shouting.*

*My dad is back and I've to go with him. I don't want to go. I don't want to go back to the bugs in my bed, back to the hitting. I want to be with my friends. I want to stay at my school. I'm given a packed lunch every day. It has crisps in it. Nobody ever gave me crisps before. I want to have shiny shoes and an ironed shirt. But I have to go. He has a new house with his girlfriend.*

*Another new school, another set of friends to make. I feel alone again.*

*I didn't see it until it was too late. I just felt my legs go from under me as SHE caught me full in the stomach.*

*I've been in this room for about five days now. SHE lets me go to school but after that I'm not allowed to leave it. Sometimes SHE gives me food and sometimes SHE doesn't. Sometimes I sit on the windowsill and watch the other children playing outside. Sometimes I watch them going out with their mums. I wish I had a mum. I wish my mum would hold my hand.*

*I like to read. It passes the time. I don't know when I learned to read; I just always remember being able to do it. I read about the 'Famous Five'. They get biscuits and orange juice. I wish I could have biscuits and orange juice. I like to travel to other worlds in my mind. When I read, life becomes beautiful and peaceful. The world is full of children who drink juice and eat biscuits and go on wild adventures. There is no hitting in that world.*

*'You're useless. Nobody likes you, you and your spastic sister. Your mother hated you. That's why she left you. Your dad hates you. I hate you.'*

*'Get your head out of that book. What are you reading? Famous Five? I'll give you a famous five punches in the head. You're useless. Just like your father.'*

*Sometimes I just wish SHE would die.*

*I don't know where my dad is. I'm hungry.*

*Some people come and take us away. I'm staying with a family I don't know. I don't know where my sister is. They won't tell me. Just another family - just another set of faces I'll soon have to forget.*

*Dad's back again. This is my life. What's the point of it? Maybe God hates me too. Maybe he thinks I'm useless.*

*I can't breathe. SHE's strangling me. Dad's lost his wages on the horses again. He hasn't come home. It's my fault. I'm useless. I wonder why my mother left me.*

*At night I look at the stars and dream that I'm in a far-off place. I wonder what other boys are doing in other countries at this precise moment in time. I wonder how many other people are looking out of their windows and wishing for a better life.*

*My sister is being beaten again. I can hear her screaming in the other room. I think it's because she's a 'spastic'. They call her that a lot. She's useless too. Nobody likes her either. I wonder why nobody likes us.*

*I write to my mother today. I tell her how much I love England and how happy I am. SHE makes me write lies. As a reward I don't get beaten today. I can't remember the last time that happened.*

*My sister is being beaten again. I don't know why. I don't care. It isn't me. It isn't me. I want to be brave and stand up for her. I just stand and watch, glad that it isn't me.*

*My uncle comes to visit. I've never seen him before. He gives me money. SHE takes it from me when he goes. Next time he comes he brings me a football. SHE takes it from me and gives it to her own son. Next time my uncle comes they have an argument. He hits her so hard SHE flies over a table. He's my hero. I go to bed and dream of hitting her so hard SHE flies over a table too.*

## My secret

*Sometimes I wonder if everybody in my class is beaten but they just don't talk about it. It's a secret we all keep from each other and from our teacher.*

*Sometimes a social worker visits me and asks me questions. Am I happy? What does that mean? I'm happy at school. I'm happy reading and writing and learning. I don't want school to finish. Sometimes I wish I could live at school. But every day I have to go home, back to the room, back to the shouting and screaming and hitting.*

*I decide to run away from home. I read about it in a book. I could have an amazing adventure and meet all sorts of people. They would be nice to me and I could start a new life. I get to the end of our road and hide in a bush. I read my book and fall asleep. I'm cold and hungry so I go home. I'm beaten. But at least now I'm only hungry.*

*I run away again. This time I get into the town centre but the police pick me up. I pretend not to know my name, but they find it out anyway. I beg them not to take me back. They do. I think SHE's paid them to bring me back. I'm beaten.*

*'You're useless. You're thick. You're stupid. Nobody likes you. I hate you. Your mother hates you. Your dad hates you. You'll never amount to anything in your whole life.'*

*Today I took my 11+ exam. I had to spell the word 'vegetable'. I hope I spelt it right. I can't remember. Maybe I am useless.*

*We've just had our 11+ exam results. They're in envelopes and the teacher tells us to take them straight home. On the way home I ask*

God to let me pass. I promise that I'll never ask him for another thing again as long as I pass this exam. I haven't talked to God for a long time. I used to pray that he would make the hitting stop, but he never did. He must really hate me too. I hope that he'll listen to me just this once.

I give her the envelope. SHE's drunk again. SHE reads the note and then looks at me. I've passed! I was stupid and useless and everybody hated me but I didn't care. I'd passed! That night SHE beat me and beat me and beat me. SHE dragged me around the room by my hair. SHE kicked me. SHE spat on me. SHE head-butted me. I staggered to my room. It was the sweetest beating of my life.

I passed! I passed!! I sat in my room and laughed and laughed and laughed. I jumped on my bed. I punched the air. SHE never called me stupid again.

There's an open day at the Grammar school I'll be going to. I have to wear a uniform with a tie and a blazer. The people from the social pay for it. It's an all-boys' school. It's Heath Grammar School. I feel proud.

I don't have any gym kit. All the other boys have shorts and shirts and nice new trainers. I have to play sports in my new grey trousers. I get grass on the knees playing rugby. At home time all the other boys are picked up by their parents. I walk into town and take the bus home by myself. When I get home I'm beaten for getting my trousers dirty. I daren't tell her that I need some kit.

I don't fit in at this stupid school. All the other boys have nice clothes and watches with calculators on! Their parents drive nice cars. They have clean clothes, pressed trousers and smart white shirts. I wish I had a crease in my trousers. Nobody irons my clothes. Nobody washes my shirt. I only have one pair of trousers and one shirt. Sometimes they aren't washed for ages. Sometimes I do them myself in the bathroom sink.

My shoes wear out and I stuff card covered in plastic bread bags on to the inside of the soles. I shuffle my feet in the playground so nobody sees.

'Non-uniform day tomorrow, lads. Don't forget.'

The dreaded words. I don't have any nice clothes to wear. I only have my school trousers and my shirt. Some of the other boys line up at the gate and laugh at me for being a 'gypsy'. I feel so alone.

I've a pain in my stomach. It hurts so much. They send me home from school. When I get home SHE is there with her friends. They call for a doctor but SHE just laughs at me. I try to sit in a chair but SHE throws me on the floor.

'There's nothing wrong with you that a good beating wouldn't cure!'

SHE kicks me in the stomach. I pass out. The doctor comes. He calls an ambulance. They put the lights and the siren on. I feel very excited. I'm having my own adventure just like the Famous Five.

I've to have an operation because I have appendicitis. The doctor goes away and SHE hits me in the head and tells me to stop crying. Some people come and take me away on a trolley. I am scared. I am alone.

I wake up and my dad's there holding my hand.

Lots of people from my school come to visit me in hospital. It makes me feel good. My dad visits me and sometimes SHE comes as well. After a week I'm allowed to go home. Because I still can't walk very far my dad fetches me and we leave in a taxi. I'm allowed to lie on the couch and watch television. I feel like a king.

The next day when my dad goes to work SHE makes me go to the shop. I have to buy seven pints of milk and ten pounds of potatoes. The pain in my side makes me cry. A lady stops and helps me to carry the stuff to my door. When I get in I'm beaten for not carrying it myself. My scar starts to bleed.

SHE throws an ornament at me today, a little brass one. It hits me on the head. I'm bleeding. Dad walks in and looks at me bleeding on the floor and then at her standing over me with a broom handle. He goes berserk and throws her out into the street. He tells her it's over. There's screaming and swearing. I've given up hoping that I'll never see her again for it's a scene I've seen them play hundreds of times before. Every time SHE's back the next day.

*SHE hasn't come back yet. It's been two days. My dad has been playing games with my sister and me. We played 'Operation' and 'Tip the waiter'.*

*I live in fear of her turning up at any moment to beat us for daring to have fun and for staying up until 6 o'clock to watch the television. I daren't go out to play in case SHE does come back and I'm not there.*

*But SHE's never coming back.*
*I will never be beaten again.*
*I am thirteen years old.*

# 2

# LIFE BEGINS OR DOES IT?

They say that life begins at forty. Who they are? I have no idea. But whoever they are, they're wrong. For me, at least, life began at thirteen. I suddenly woke up one day and realised that there should have been more to my life than making the choice between covering my testicles or protecting my head in the daily round of beatings.

I don't know if I made the discovery straight away or if it came gradually. One day I just woke up and things were different. I got out of bed and realised that I was angry. I was angry at this woman, angry at my dad, angry at the world, angry at myself. There were so many people and so many things that I was angry with that I didn't know where to begin. I felt so impotent and helpless. I wanted somebody to suffer, to pay for what SHE did to me. I wanted her to die. At the very least, I wanted her to suffer and be humiliated. But SHE wouldn't suffer and SHE wouldn't die. I would suffer. I would suffer for the torment of all those years, and not one person could do a single thing about it. The realisation of this drove me to frustrated tears. What about justice? What about fairness? What was I supposed to do with all of my anger? What does a thirteen-year-old boy do with this swirl of emotions that he is barely able to comprehend?

Sometimes I walked in the fields behind my house and thought for hours and hours. I remember often thinking that maybe it hadn't happened after all, that it had simply been my overactive imagination. But it had happened, and it was real. Somebody out there had to be responsible. Who? I didn't know. I still don't. It was simply life, the way of the world. It was just how the cards had fallen. My life was a cliché and I just had to get on with it.

Sometimes I looked at my friends at school. They had clean uniforms, shoes without holes and money for the tuck shop. They swapped football cards and did all the things they were supposed to do. And I wanted to be them. I wanted to go to the school gate, jump in the back of my dad's car and drive home to my mother for tea. But I wasn't them; I was me. I was the scruffy kid with holes in his shoes that hardly saw his dad, who didn't have a mother, and who was lucky if he got any tea at all. This was my life and it wasn't fair. But why should it be? Why should anything make sense in a senseless world?

Nobody stopped to think about me. Nobody commiserated with my awful experience. They were all too busy. Having the complete England team for the '86 World Cup was crucial stuff. Making sure they had the right trainers and the right haircut, chasing teenage girls - what could be more important than that?

My teachers were more concerned about my maths homework than with me. I wanted them all to stop, just for a minute, and at least acknowledge my grief. I wanted somebody to at least say 'Mez, what happened to you was awful, a crime. I'm sorry.' But nobody did and nobody ever would. So I would make them listen. At fourteen years of age I took a decision that would impact on my life for the better part of a decade. I would simply refuse to follow the rules. I would simply refuse to let *them* tell me what to do and how to do it. I had had enough of adults ordering me around and trying to control my life. I might have been helpless about the past, but I vowed that I would never allow myself to be in that position in the future. Nobody was going to order me around any more.

I wouldn't realise the irony of this period of my life for another fifteen years. This woman leaving was the greatest thing that had ever happened to me. No more pain, no more suffering, no more fear. Yet it turned out, at one level, to be the worst thing that could possibly happen. I could never have guessed it at the time, but it led to a downward spiral of self destruction that lasted for the next decade.

*A friend of mine was stabbed to death today. He wasn't a particularly good friend. We had shared the odd cigarette and a laugh. The girl who did it used to be my girlfriend. She stabbed him in the chest with a kitchen knife. He crawled into the street with a knife wound in his chest and lay there dying. He died in a car on the way to hospital. He was fifteen years old. His life just ebbed away in the back of a grotty old car and there was nothing anybody could have done to help him. He had to face death alone and we were just helpless bystanders.*

It was reported in the national press the next day as a 'Romeo and Juliet' crime. They made it sound romantic and exciting, but the reality was that he was a boy who wet himself and drowned in his own blood as the life was sucked out of him. There was nothing remotely romantic about it at all.

Two friends of the family were knocked down and killed. I read about it in the paper when I was on holiday. As they left a pub a taxi mounted the kerb and smashed into them. They were killed instantly. The papers said it was romantic how two teenage sweethearts had gone together. There was nothing remotely romantic about it at all. They both went through the windscreen and were smashed to pieces by an underage driver without a license.

My social worker is dead. He committed suicide. He fed a pipe from his car exhaust in through the car window and turned the engine on. One day he's telling me how to work through my 'issues' and the next day he's dead. I feel cheated. How could he help me when he couldn't even help himself?

That was the first time I consciously questioned life. More than that, it was when I began to realise that life didn't last forever. I began to question my own mortality. I thought I believed in God. But who was God? What did he have to do with me? What had he ever done for me? Was there a reason for all this madness? Did there even have to be a reason? I didn't know why we were here and it seemed that nobody else did either. Maybe God was someone we made up to make us feel better about ourselves. I went to the funerals but found no comfort there. We sang songs and we committed them to a god that none of us ever seemed to talk about.

## Change of direction

*School, which had once been my only refuge, now became the bane of my life. I lost all motivation to study and do well. I took perverse pleasure in handing in work that I knew to be wrong. I became uncooperative and sullen and grew to resent my teachers and fellow students more and more. What was the point of it all anyway? To get a good job? To earn lots of money? We were all going to die and it all seemed like a momentous waste of time and effort. What good will a job and money do when we're dead?*

*I threw a chair at my teacher today. He tried to embarrass me in class and I lost my temper. It hit him on the head. I don't know who was more surprised, him or me. It felt good and gave me a sense of control over my life. The sensation and outrage that caused in the school was overwhelming. But at least he was a man and could defend himself. Where was all this outrage when I was being kicked and beaten and spat on?*

*I leave school hating the place and all the teachers in it.*

*I've just started my first job. It's in a big factory on the outskirts of town. A little mini bus picks us up at our front doors and drops us off at work. How cool is that? I can make a few quid and I don't have to worry about school anymore. The place is the absolute pits! Most of the windows are broken and there's no heating. I'm taken to a table and told to begin sticking badges on birthday cards. I've to do a minimum of a thousand a day. I last three days. How can people work like this?*

*I've got another job! I'm working for a kitchen unit manufacturer. My job is to stand at the end of a production line and stack cabinet doors in piles of sixty on to wooden pallets that are then wheeled away to be shrink wrapped. It's backbreaking, mind-numbing work. Most of the people here seem quite happy with it. I spend most of my time daydreaming of bigger and better things. And I last six weeks.*

*I decide to go to the local college to study business and finance. I pick the subject because it sounds interesting - it sounds like a sure fire way to make money. Oh, and because it's about the only course that I can take with my qualifications.*

*My class is full of the usual wide-eyed boys dreaming of being the next Richard Branson. There are two public school boys in the class who like playing three-card brag at break times. It's so easy to fleece them that it's embarrassing. But it's not so embarrassing that I don't do it! If the world is full of clueless muppets like them, then sooner or later I'm going to hit the jackpot. I get bored and quit after a few months.*

*Shoes! Everybody needs shoes. How hard can it be to sell shoes? Not very, as it turns out. But what they didn't put in the job description was the kind of person I had to work for. I thought that three weeks was a laudable effort on my part.*

*I'm going to be a trainee accountant! How cool is that! I'll be making big bucks soon!*

*Man, this accountancy lark is boring with a capital B. One day I looked at my boss in his Marks & Spencer suit and thought, 'I don't want to be like that'. I left for lunch and never went back.*

I always wanted to be a journalist so, when the chance came to join a real live magazine on a government scheme, I jumped at it. I was very nervous when I went for my interview, but it went very well and they said I could join them. The magazine was called *'The Northern*

*Star.'* It was a left-wing weekly with a print run of about 10,000. It was dead trendy. It was run as a co-operative, which meant everybody had a say in business meetings. They were all called Tarquin and Brandon etc., and the woman at the desk across from me used to have a girlfriend who came to collect her at lunch-time. Sometimes they kissed right there in the office. Nobody said anything because they were all so radical!

*I've been made redundant. It seems like we were too trendy for some politician or other. We must have been - he sued us.*

*I'm nearly eighteen years old and I feel like a complete failure. What am I going to do with my life? I need a new challenge.*

*I decide that I will form my own magazine with the help of some friends. After much talk and preparation we call this new magazine the 'Calderdale Commotion'. We name it Calderdale after the borough in which we live. The local Council and the Youth and Community section has agreed to finance the venture, and our initial print run is going to be 10,000. The magazine will be aimed at the 16 - 24 year old age group. We want to deal with issues like drugs, AIDS, joyriding, prison etc. Our aim is to try to educate young people by making them aware of issues.*

The Lord Mayor and a number of other dignitaries attend the launch. I'm interviewed by the local newspaper and on BBC radio. I feel like a celebrity. At last my life has direction.

# 3

# THE BIG BAD WORLD

'*What do you mean that you've had an abortion? What have you done that for? We're not too young. You've murdered my baby!*'

*I watch, fascinated, as he sticks the Rizla papers together. Then comes the cigarette tobacco, and finally he pulls out the cannabis. It looks like a little lump of plasticine. He burns the end of it with his lighter until it begins to smoke and give off a pungent smell. It crumbles in his fingers and he mixes it liberally into the tobacco. He licks the Rizla and rolls it together. Next he tears a small strip of paper from his cigarette packet. He rolls it into a tight cylindrical shape and slides it into one end whilst twisting up the other. Finally, he pops it into my mouth and lights it.*

'*Just inhale deeply,*' *he says,* '*and enjoy.*'

*My head is spinning and I can't get my mind to work properly. Everything is out of focus. Words and pictures and ideas are running around my head at one hundred miles an hour. I can't keep up. I slump back on the floor.*

'*Hey, Mez is throwing a whitey!*'

'*Hey, Mez. Get it together, man.*'

*A whitey, otherwise known as paranoia. Man, I hate this cannabis stuff. I absolutely hate it. I hate the taste, the smell and the sensation of not being in control. I gotta stop smoking this rubbish.*

'Man, I've got the munchies. Anybody else got the munchies?'

'Yeh, I've got the munchies.'

'Me too.'

There was no warning with the munchies. When they came you had to satisfy them. Sometimes at two or three in the morning we would all suddenly get the urge for a packet of cheese and onion crisps. The urge would soon become an obsession, and sometimes we would walk miles and miles to try and find a petrol station that was open so that we could stack up on goodies. For a while it became our Saturday night ritual.

'Smoking the weed is OK but have you ever tried speed?'

'OK then, why not.'

I looked at the white powdery substance in my hand. It had been folded into a small packet using the pages of a glossy magazine, and then wrapped in Clingfilm. This was known as a 'wrap'.

'So what do I have to do?'

'Well, you can 'bomb' it (pour it into a cigarette paper, screw it up and swallow it), snort it or, if you're feeling adventurous, you can dig (inject) it.'

I decide to bomb it.

'Is that it? I don't feel anything.'

'Give it time, Mez. It'll kick in soon.'

'Nothing. I'm feeling nothing.'

'Here, double up the dose.'

'You sure?'

'Yeh. You'll be fine, Mate.'

I think I feel it in my toes first. A small, tingling sensation, a growing euphoria, and a feeling of wellbeing that suddenly sweeps up my legs, arms, body and finally explodes in my head. I feel wired. My senses are heightened. I feel like I could take on the world. I'm in control. I like this. No, I love it.

I've been high for three days in a row. I haven't eaten and I've hardly slept. I feel dirty and tired. Why am I doing this?

'Ever been to a rave?'

'No.'

'Wanna come to one?'
'Yeh.'
'Here, try this.'
'What is it?'
'An E.'
'OK.'

One day I left home to go to a rave and I suppose I just never went back.

### Living the dream!

*There's no lock on the door so we jam it shut with a plank of wood. The curtains are drawn and there's no electricity. The candles give the place an eerie feel. I can't see the floor because of the needles and rubbish. The whole place smells. There's a mattress on the floor. I flake out and try to get some sleep.*

*I'm thirsty. I go to the kitchen to get a drink of water but there's somebody in there. I watch as he injects something into the veins between his fingers. It's over so quickly that he's obviously a veteran. Somebody else I've never seen before is lying on the floor. A needle hangs out of a vein in his arm and a line of blood trickles down from it. What am I doing here? Where is my life going? Thoughts pass through my mind but are gone before I can analyse them.*

*It's New Years Eve and there's a big rave on in Bradford. There's a lot to do. We've to go and score for a start. We pick up 200 LSD tabs, 100 Es and a couple of ounces of speed. We might as well make a few quid while we're there. They reckon there's going to be thousands there so we'll have no bother getting shot of them.*

*How mad is this? 3000 people rocking the place! I drop an E and some speed and wait for the party to really start.*

*I can't feel my legs! I'm flying! I just feel so much love! How can this be wrong? How can this be illegal? Just feel it!*

*I never want this to end!*

*My head is mashed, battered, fried. What am I doing? I haven't slept for days. I can't think straight. What am I doing? I don't even know what I'm taking half the time. It's not so much fun any more.*

*I cut up an ounce of speed with detergent powder today. What's that going to do to people? What am I doing? Who cares anyway?*

   *'What's it all about, life?'*
   *'About getting high.'*
   *'Seriously.'*
   *'Who cares, man? Get this down your neck and forget about it.'*

*I can't just sit around in this squat all day taking drugs. There's got to be more to life than this, surely. Why won't my friends discuss it? Why can't we face the truth that our lives are going nowhere? I feel like we are missing something important, but I don't know what it is. I want to ask questions, but I don't know what questions to ask. I don't know who to ask. I want answers, but nobody has any. Everybody has ideas and theories, but nobody has answers.*

*'Don't you want more from life?'*
   *'Like what?'*
   *'I dunno. Surely there has to be a purpose to it all?'*
   *'Why? Why should there be a purpose to it all?'*
   *'I dunno. I just feel like we're missing out on something better than this.'*
   *'Life is for living, Mez. For getting high, for getting girls. For living right on the edge. There IS no point.'*
   *'You honestly believe that?'*
   *'I dunno. Give it a rest. You're doing my napper in.'*
*I can't keep on doing this. I want to get away from it all. I want to start again.*
   *Who are all these people? What am I doing here? I have to get out of here now.*

# 4

# THINKING BACK

*M*y palms are sweating. I'm sure that he's watching me. No, he's serving a customer. No, he's looking again. No, he's serving someone.

Now's my chance. Yes, I've done it! I run outside quickly and count my booty. One … two … thirteen. Thirteen white chocolate mice. All hail the master criminal. I am ten years old.

The police came round to the house today while I was washing up. They wanted me to 'help them with their enquiries.'

I have to go to the station with my step mum because I'm only twelve. They give me a caution for assault. Basically, some fat copper comes in the room and gives it the tough guy routine and I try to act as contrite as possible. It's all over in ten minutes. How dumb are this lot!

There was a mini riot on the estate tonight. It was a good buzz! There were coppers everywhere, fighting all these punk rockers. One punk got his head shoved through a window by an absolutely enormous copper. Somebody set a squad car on fire. It was class!

Golden rule number one: the police are the enemy.

Golden rule number two: you don't know anything.

Golden rule number three: you didn't see a thing.

It's as simple as that. It doesn't matter whether they want to know your name or ask you the time. Your name is Jesus and it's time to get *a watch. You've seen nothing, you've heard nothing, you've never heard of anybody. You simply don't know.*

*They are the rules. Never break them. Never think about breaking them. There are no exceptions to the rules. Ever. The police are the enemy. Grasses are the enemy. Grasses don't last long on our estate. We know who they are and where they live. Coppers are scum and our job is to be as unco-operative and obstructive as possible. It's a game to be played at every opportunity. We are brilliant at it. Absolutely first class.*

*There's a big group out tonight. There's got to be 30 at least.*

    *'Hey, Mez. What you up to?'*

    *'Absolutely nada.'*

    *'Got any gear?'*

    *'Nah. I've got a few quid though. Maybe we could get a five spot.'*

    *'Nice one.'*

*Every night it's the same old, same old thing.*

    *'Why don't we ring the busies and say some kids are racing a stolen car on the streets by the library.'*

    *'Yeah, and hopefully they'll send a crew up and we'll have a right chase.'*

    *'If we can get them to chase us up by the building site we'll be able to brick 'em from the roof.'*

    *'I like it.'*

    *'The old Spar shop is definitely not belled up.'*

    *'How do you know?'*

    *'I checked it out today. I tell you, it's easy.'*

    *'How're we gonna get in?'*

    *We'll just smash the front window and climb in.'*

    *'We need two of us to go in and fill as many bin bags as we can with fags and booze, and somebody to keep an eye out for the busies.'*

    *'Why not? It'll be a good crack.'*

Yes, it was a stupid idea. But the higher we got the more invincible we thought we were. We were nicked, banged to rights with over a grand worth of booze and cigarettes. We did the job and got out all right. It was just the getaway that we didn't think about, the bit after we got out the window and ran back to a friend's house. He only lived about two hundred yards across the road. We were so high we didn't notice the fact that one of the bags of cigarettes had split and left a trail all the way up to his front door. I think the police were too busy laughing at us to read us our rights. That little episode cost me forty hours community service and about £400 worth of fines.

*'How many of them are there?'*
*'Dunno. Twenty maybe?'*
*'What we gonna do now then?'*
*'Let's just go for it. You take the big fella up the front and we'll just see what happens.'*

We took a bit of a beating that day. There were about five of us and we got absolutely battered. It was one of the few times that I was glad when the police eventually turned up. I had been hit in the legs with an iron bar and one of my friends had a dart stuck in the back of his head. We were in a real mess. But it cemented our friendship. It gave us a sense of camaraderie, of belonging, and I liked it. I felt accepted for the first time in my life. I didn't feel so alone in the world. But revenge was not long in coming.

*'That's one of them, isn't it?'*
*'I think so.'*
*He hasn't seen us. Let's just do him.'*
*'OK. Who's got the cheese wire?'*
*'Let's go.'*

## More Trouble

*End terraced, semi detached, detached. Those were the big three. No alarm and easy rear access. If it backed on to a field or some wasteland, that was a bonus. Patio doors were a winner because we could be in and out quicker than through an ordinary window. Storms are a burglar's best friend. Failing that, high winds and rain. Anything to disguise the noise of breaking glass or a door being jimmied. Another good trick is to break a car window a couple of hundred yards down the road and let the alarm go off. That's guaranteed to cause a fuss, and by the time anybody knows what's happening we've been and gone!*

It started off as a night out for about ten of us. We'd been to a club in town and were on our way back on the bus. We were all in high spirits. In fact, we'd been making so much noise that the bus driver stopped the bus and phoned the police.

*'Right, off the bus. I've had enough!'*
  *'I'm not getting off, you muppet!'*
  *'Well, I'm not getting off unless I get a refund!'*
  *'Stick your refund. I'm not getting off!'*
  *'Well, I've rung the police. They are on their way.'*
  *'So. Let 'em come.'*

Two of them turned up. As soon as they came upstairs we knew there'd be trouble because the pair of them were as bent as they come. They had nicked a couple of us before and on more than one occasion we'd had a sly dig in the back of a police car. I was sitting near the front when they got on and they didn't see me because they headed straight for the back seats.

*'Off!'*
  *'Why?'*
  *'We ain't done nothing!'*
  *'If you hadn't done anything we wouldn't be here, would we? Now off!'*
  *'Nah.'*
  *'Off!'*
  *'Make us.'*
  *'If you don't move then we're going to nick you.'*
  *"What, all of us?'*
  *'All of you.'*
  *'Don't think so.'*
  *All of a sudden one of them takes a swing and hits my young sister in the face. Taking his lead, the other pounces on a lad sitting next to*

her. *All hell breaks loose. We charge up the bus and lay into them. They quickly back off and call for assistance.*

*The bus is at a complete standstill and all the rest of the passengers jump off. Within minutes police are everywhere. There are about ten of them on the top deck with more waiting downstairs. One taunts and hits my friend in the face. I charge at him and begin hitting him but I'm knocked to the floor by one of his friends and they drag me away from the rest of my group.*

*They throw me down the stairs into the arms of their friends who beat me with their truncheons, fists … anything. I'm bundled into a car and held down by a couple of policemen and taken to the station. I'm bleeding from the head and have bruises everywhere, but they claim that I inflicted the injuries on myself during the course of my arrest!*

*'Are you Merrix William Alexander McConnell?'*

*'Yeh.'*

*'Yes, Your Honour.'*

*'Yes, Your Honour.'*

*'In the matter of the Crown versus Merrix William Alexander McConnell, I find the defendant guilty on three charges of assault against the police and a further charge of disturbing the peace.'*

Sometimes we went through the telephone directory and phoned people to see if they were in. If nobody answered, we paid a visit to see if it was worth burgling. Other times we picked a house that looked ripe and I knocked on the door and asked for some fictional person. If somebody answered, I'd just pretend I had the wrong street name. If nobody came to the door, we were in business.

We weren't fancy. Straight in, and the televisions, videos and stereos went first. We'd get them out and stash them somewhere. Then, if we had time, we'd go back and look for valuables. If not, it was no big deal. A decent television, video and stereo would get us a hundred quid. Five of them a night was easy money. Ten minutes per job and that was five hundred quid for less than an hour's work.

Sweet! Yet after the cut I would be lucky if I had a fiver and a packet of fags. A lot of risk for peanuts really. But the buzz was worth it.

*We've been chipping away at this brickwork for nearly five hours now. The hole is only just big enough for me to squeeze through. I'll have to be quick because he opens up to do the papers in an hour. I should be OK as long as I crawl under the infrared lines. Just the fags and any spare cash.*

*The busies are coming! I'm gone.*

*All that for nothing but at least we didn't get nicked this time!*

*Sometimes I feel bad for nicking people's stuff. But I only rob from those who can afford it. Most of the time I just don't think about it. I can't do this forever though, can I?*

'About five o'clock on a Saturday night he takes the cash box up the road and puts it in the bank. Must be at least a grand in it.'

'What, from selling shoes?'

'I'm telling you. It's manic on a Saturday. It's got to be a grand, easy.'

"What if he puts up a fight?"

'No chance. He's a right muppet. A quick punch to the head and he'll be gone. Trust me.'

'Why don't you do it if it's so easy?'

'Cos they'll clock me straight away. I'll be the first person they question. They will never even think of you.'

'OK, I'll check it out.'

*He bottled it.*

*Why am I doing this? There must be more to life than this? Moving from one blag to the next. I don't want to do this anymore.*

'Wanna buy a card?'

"What you got?"

'Visas, mainly.'

'How old?'

'Couple of hours, max.'

"How much?"

'Fifty quid.'

*'Thirty.'*
*'Done.'*
*Easy money.*

I was sweating big time. I was sure the police were going to jump out at any minute and nick me. The cashier looked at me in my shirt and tie. He looked and looked. I held his eye. He handed over the brown envelope stuffed with £50 notes – £2,190 to be exact. I turned and walked calmly out of the bank. One false passport and a short plane ride later I was in the Costa del Sol. No more drugs, no more crime. This was going to be the start of a new and better life.

# 5

# NEW BEGINNINGS AND OLD 'CONTINUINGS'

'*Let's have a drink to celebrate.*'
    '*Celebrate what?*'
  '*New beginnings.*'
  '*Yeh, OK.*'
  '*What about a bit of coke just to liven things up a bit?*'
  "*No, ta.*'
  '*Come on. Just a quick snifter for old times sake.*'
  '*Yeh, OK then.*'

'*Where's all the money?*'
  '*Gone.*'
  '*What do you mean, gone? How can it be gone? We've only been here for ten days.*'
  '*It's gone. Booze, drugs, food. I dunno. I just know that it's gone.*'
  '*Stuff that then. I'm not sticking around here without any cash. I'm off.*'
  '*Me too. You're on your own, Mez.*'
  *They fly back to England and leave me penniless and homeless. So much for new beginnings. I've never felt so alone.*

'*Alright, Mate. Where you from?*'
  '*Yorkshire. You?*'
  '*Swindon. Got any gear?*'
  '*Yeh. How much do you want?*'

'You got anywhere to crash, Mez?'
'Nah. I'm just crashing out on the beach most nights.'
'Come and crash at our place then.'
'Yeh?'
'Yeh.'
'Sweet.'

'How much to hire a car, Mate?'
'How much? That'll do.'
'Do you wanna buy a car, Mate?'
'It's bent. We ripped it off from the south. They don't know it's missing yet though because it's not due back till tomorrow.'

'Need any gear, Mate? Pills, hash, coke, speed, tabs. We got them all, Mate.'
'Quick, it's the busies. Get rid quick!'
'Run!'

'Mez, we gotta get out of here. If the police get us we're done, Mate.'
'That's OK for you. If I go back to Yorkshire, I'm well and truly nicked.'
'Then come back to Swindon with us. We'll sort you out. No problem.'
'Alright then. Nice one lads.'
'No probs, Mate.'

'Sorry, Mate. My old man says you can't crash here anymore.'
'What do mean, 'sorry, Mate'? I've got no money, no clothes and nowhere to live. What am I supposed to do now?'
'Go home, Mate.'
'Yeh, good idea, Einstein. I'll just go home because I'm sure the police have forgotten all about me.'
'Sorry, Mate. Nothing I can do.'
'Yeh, whatever.'

This can't be happening to me. What am I going to do? I've got no money and nowhere to live. Homeless. Man, I can't be homeless.

Man, it's cold out here tonight. I can't keep walking around in circles or someone will ring the police on me. Maybe I should just phone my dad and go home and face the music. Nah. I don't think so.

*Homeless people are peasants, junkies, sad, down-and-outs.*
*I've never felt so scared. Or alone.*

*He can't be much more than seventeen. Lying there in his own vomit. The stink is unbearable so I get to my feet and move further down the station. The old man across from me grins and offers me a banana. I take it. It's cold so I get up and walk around.*

*I kicked the back door in. The wood was rotten and it went first time. It must have been empty for ages because it smelled terrible. I don't care. It's dry and warm. What am I doing?*

*'Hello Dad? It's me.'*

*'What? Yeh, I'm sound. Doing well for myself. Got a job and everything.*

*What? In a factory. Yeh, I've got a nice place. And a girlfriend. Life's sweet.'*

*Sometimes I almost believed my own lies.*

## There is no God

*What's the point of all this? I'm hungry. Maybe if I just lie down and go to sleep I'll never wake up. That'd be nice, never to wake up again. I wonder what it would feel like to just drift away. No one would miss me. Some people might cry for a bit, but that would be it. I'd just be gone. I'd just be a memory. Then pretty soon I'd be forgotten and nobody would know that I was ever even here on this miserable planet.*

*My stomach hurts. I can't tell whether it's from the hunger or from the hopelessness of it all. There's no one out there. Who are we kidding? There is no God. We're on our own. Nobody sees us or hears us or understands us. The world is living in denial. We're all alone.*

*'Why don't you come and crash on the floor at my house?'*

*'Nice one. It's better than the hole I'm living in now.'*

*'Least it'll give you an address and you can sign on for the old rock and roll (dole).'*

*Got my first dole cheque today. Bought some new clothes and scored some Billy. Thought I might as well have a little celebration.*

'What do you think the meaning of life is?'

'Who knows? Are you marrying that spliff or what? Pass it on.'

'But don't you ever think about it?'

'Nah. Life's for living not thinking.'

'You're telling me that you never think about this stuff?'

'Sometimes. But what's the point. Nobody really knows the answers. So we might as well just get on with it.'

*I've met a girl. She's very nice. She makes me feel better about myself and she's a good crack when we get high. All the essential ingredients for a potential wife!*

'What do you mean you're mum's made you have an abortion? How can she make you have an abortion? So what if I haven't got a job or a proper place to live. So what? Does that mean you can murder my baby?'

*It can happen at any time and without any warning. One minute I'm OK and the next I can't breathe. I get all hot and sweaty and my heart starts pumping hard. It feels like it's going to burst out of my chest. This is it. I'm having a heart attack! I'm going to die right here in the street and nobody can do anything about it. Nobody can help me. I'm going to die alone.*

*I feel empty inside. Dead. Something is missing and I don't know what it is. Why can't anybody answer my questions? Somebody out there must be able to help me.*

# 6

# ONWARD AND DOWNWARD

'*Hello, Son.*'
    '*Hello.*'
  '*Ina.*'
  '*OK.*'

*She took my hand and there were tears in her eyes. I just looked at her. There was no emotion. No feeling of attachment, no relief. Nothing. Just a tiny woman with light brown hair who had given birth to me twenty years ago. But all my hopes were pinned on her. Surely now my life would take on new meaning.*

  '*I'll just get your bags.*'

*She's got a husband and three children of her own. What am I doing here? She's got her own life. I'm a mistake from long ago. I've no place here. What was I thinking? That we would run into each other's arms and all would be well with the world? Possibly. I don't really know. I just wanted answers. Why? Why had she left us to suffer like that? Why did she leave us? Did she love us? Me? Did she love me? She doesn't have a clue. She's more mixed up than I am. I won't find my redemption in her. The realisation that she can't help me hits like a thunderbolt. She doesn't have any answers. She doesn't even understand the questions. I had pinned all my hopes on her and it was for nothing. I'm going. There's nothing here for me but bad memories for her. She looks more alone than I feel. Now what am I going to do? Who will help me now?*

'What do you need, Mez?'
  'Got any Billy?'
  'Yeh, how much?'
  'A gram?'
  'Sorted. A tenner.'

'Excuse me.'
  'Yeh, what?'
  'We just wondered if you'd like to play a game of football?'
  'Yeh, alright.'

That's how I met them, the Christians. The Bible bashers, gimps, freaks. Take your pick. They just turned up one day out of the blue. I wasn't too sure at first. Maybe they weren't Christians. Maybe they were the police. They had hired the gym in the Centre and invited us in to play football with them. I was highly suspicious. People just don't turn up out of nowhere and ask you to play football, do they?

'Hands up if you've ever heard of Jesus Christ?'
  *Is this guy for real or what? Hands up if you've ever heard of Jesus? I knew there was some catch. Do you want to come and play football? They're Bible bashers! They're trying to convert us and brainwash us into joining their group. I'm going to have to keep an eye on this lot.*
  'Jesus died for your sins.'
  *You what? Jesus died for my sins? What is this bloke on about? Jesus died for my sins? Well, that's his problem then, isn't it?*
  'Why don't you just shut up going on about God, Mate?'
  'Because he wants to have a relationship with you.'
  'You what? A relationship? What you on about, Mate? Are you off your head or what?'
  'God loves you, Mez.'
  'Well that's a real comfort when I'm sleeping on my floor tonight. If God loves me, Mate, then why does my life suck?'
  'Because of your sin.'

*'Tell you what, why don't you and I go outside and we'll see if your mighty God can stop me kicking your backside. How about that, God freak?'*

*I had another panic attack today. That's the third one this week. I can't seem to control them. Sometimes my chest tightens up and I get pains in my arms and can't breathe. I curl up into a ball and pray that it will go away. God, please help me!*

*God loves us. Jesus died for us. God wants to have a relationship with us. We need to turn from our sins if we want to go to heaven and avoid hell.*

*Jesus, Jesus, Jesus!*

*Can't this lot play another tune? It's doing my head in! I can't sleep at night thinking about this Jesus. What if it's all true? It can't be. Yeh, but what if it is? There's no way I'm joining the gimpo brigade!*

*'Do you think there's a heaven and a hell?'*

*'Dunno.'*

*'But what if there is?'*

*'There isn't.'*

*'How can you be so sure?'*

*'I can't.'*

*'Doesn't it even bother you a bit what these people are saying?'*

*'Nah, not really. I just ignore them. They can say what they like as long as I get to play footie.'*

*Sometimes I'm nearly convinced by these guys. I mean, they are so into it. They are so excited about it all. I have nothing in my life that gets me that excited. I have nothing in my life, full stop.*

## Six months

*'You're under arrest. Anything you say blah blah blah...'*

I just sat in the back of the police car and closed my eyes. I don't know why I did it, but it felt good. They'd been staring at me in the club all night. So I thought, why not? The big one went down first as the bottle smashed into his forehead. The smaller one fell screaming when the broken stub cut across his eyes. It was over in seconds. I turned and walked away. The police were waiting for me when I got outside. I could have escaped out the emergency doors, but I just couldn't be bothered. If I'm honest, it was a bit of a relief.

*'Do you have anything to say before sentence, Mr McConnell?'*

*'No'*

*'Very well. We sentence you to six months imprisonment.'*

*I'm not sorry. Why should I be? Six months is actually a good result for GBH and ABH. It could have been a lot worse. I go back to my cell under the court and wait for the meat wagon. I've got butterflies in my stomach. I don't know whether it's fear or adrenaline. Mostly fear, I think.*

*'What do you think, Mate?'*

*I shrug. The guy is built like a barn door and is proudly showing me the scars on his body. There are well over a hundred. Obviously some sort of crackpot. I just smile politely and hope he's in a good mood.*

*'What did you get?'*

*'Six months.'*

*He laughs. 'I've spent more than that on the toilet!'*

*'What did you get?'*

*'Ten years. Armed robbery.'*

*'Congratulations.'*

*'Cheers.'*

*'On your feet, McConnell!'*

*The cuffs cut into my wrists as I'm escorted to the minibus waiting in the courtyard. Police everywhere mock us as we get on board. There are five or six others in the same situation as me - all cuffed to a copper. Nobody speaks. We're all lost in our own thoughts.*

*'HMP Horfield? It's a holiday camp, Mate.'*

*He was in his mid thirties, scruffy with greasy hair, wild eyed and scared looking.*

*'You ever been inside before, Son?'*

*'No.'*

*'Ooh! The boys are gonna love you.' Wink, wink.*

*Prat.*

*I'm scared. I'm alone. Again.*

# 7

# BED & BREAKFAST BY ROYAL APPOINTMENT

*T*he prison looms large ahead. My heart is beating faster and faster. What's it going to be like? Will I get any trouble? Even worse, what if a homosexual takes a liking to me? What if a group of them do? The aloneness returns.

As we pull into the prison gates I quickly survey the scene around me. The whole prison is surrounded by huge walls and what seems like miles and miles of steel fencing. Once through the gate the van stops and the huge steel doors are shut behind us. In front stands another huge steel gate attached to an imposing steel fence, which runs around the inside of the wall. There's barbed wire everywhere.

The reception committee consists of about half-a-dozen prison warders (screws) and several large fierce-looking Alsatians. The van stops again once we're past the inner gate and we all get off - still cuffed to our escorts. We're led into the processing area, which is basically a wooden bench. The policeman takes the cuffs off and disappears, leaving me to sit on the bench with the rest of the guys there.

'Welcome home, girls.'

'McConnell!'

'Yeh.'

'Yes, Sir! Or yes, Boss! Understand?'

*'Yes, Boss.'*

*'Mess me about, kid, and I'll make your life a misery in here. Am I clear?'*

*'Yes, Boss. Crystal clear.'*

*'Take all your clothes off and put these on.'*

*'This is your prison number. WB0874. First time, Son? Well, obey everything I say and you'll be fine. Faff us about and we'll be letting the fairies play with you. Know what I'm saying?'*

*'Yeah.'*

*'Yes, Boss!'*

*'Yes, Boss.'*

I was locked in yet another room. More waiting. I wasn't bothered. The more time I spent there meant I'd be less time inside the actual prison. An old lag brought me some food and a plastic mug of tea. I couldn't eat. I was too nervous. I rolled another cigarette and supped the drink.

*'WB0874 McConnell!'*

*The doctor.*

*'First time, Son?'*

*'Yes.'*

*He looked up and stared at me. I stared back.*

*'Do you need anything?'*

*'No.'*

*'You sure you don't need anything to take the edge off, Son. The first night can be pretty rough.'*

*'No. Nothing.'*

### A pleasant surprise ...

*Everything was so clean. Not like I'd imagined it at all. I'd expected prisons to be dirty, awful places but this one was spotless. After what seemed like hours a group of us were led into the main prison block. I was going to B-Wing with another lad who arrived with me. I don't remember his name, but I do remember that he was given eighteen months for possession of one cannabis plant and I can remember thinking how tough a sentence that was. But I was in prison now and I had no time to worry about other people. I had to look after myself.*

After going through what seemed like dozens of steel gates we arrived on B-Wing. The wing was like a dormitory, with rows of cells on each side making a sort of T figure. It wasn't like I'd imagined at all. Again, everything was clean and tidy and very quiet. However, the screw with us told us that it was association night for our wing. Association meant that we were let out of our cells for an hour and a half and we could walk about the wing freely. We got association every five nights in Horfield. Seconds later there was a tap on the door.

'Got any burn, Mate?'
  'You what?'
  'Got any burn? You know, snout?'
  'No, Mate.'
  'Course you have.'
  'Don't know what you're talking about, Mate.'
  'Baccy? Rollies, fags?'
  'Yeh, I've got that.'
  'Bit of snout for a bit of weed?'
  'Yeh, OK.'

This place was OK. Much better than some of the places I'd been staying on the outside. My cell had bunk beds, a washbasin and even a toilet. Better than a B & B! I smoked my joint and slept well.

'Up, McConnell. You're being transferred for trial.'
  'Where?'
  'Yorkshire.'
  'But I only got here last week, Boss.'
  'I don't make the rules. Get your stuff. You're going now.'
  'Right you two. On the bus.'
  I'm already handcuffed and now I'm handcuffed again to a young lad of about eighteen or nineteen.

*'Alright, Mate?'*

*'Yeh. You?'*

*'Not bad. What you got?'*

*'Six months and a trial coming up. You?'*

*'Life. Murder.'*

*'Where you going?'*

*'Dunno. They keep moving me every six months and I don't know where I'm going till I get there.'*

*'What's this place, Boss?'*

*'Rugby Young Offenders. Doubles as a dispersal unit.'*

*It's like a train station. Every holding cell could fit ten to twenty men and has the name of its prison on the door. I'm shoved into the 'Armley Prison, Leeds' cell.*

*'You, McConnell! On your feet. We're going.'*

*By now the routine's boring - asking and answering the same questions. What else is there to say? I get on the bus and sleep.*

### ...but not for long

*This place stinks! Is that urine in the corner? And there's faeces on the walls! This place is the pits! We're crowded in like sardines here. There has to be at least fifteen of us. There's an idiot in the corner spouting off about how many burglaries he's done and how many he's got away with. A real master criminal! I think I'll just get my head down and hope nobody notices me.*

*'WB0874 McConnell.'*

*'Yeh'.*

*'Yes, Sir!'*

*The screw at the desk asks me a long list of questions: name, age, all that sort of stuff. When he gets to religion, I nearly said Muslim but I bottle it at the last minute. One old prisoner told me that if you put yourself down as a Muslim then you get chicken curry at weekends. I thought he was winding me up, but I found out later that it was true.*

*'Right, strip and stand on that yellow line. Shorts and all. Right, bend over…clean. Right, follow that yellow line and collect some clothes. Sign here for your possessions.'*

*The yellow line leads to the shower block that's staffed by some cons who hand me shoes (without laces), a shirt, a pair of socks, and a pair of jeans. I am then furnished with a plastic mug, plate, knife, fork and spoon that I'm told to keep with me at all times. I dress quickly and am shown into a very large holding cell with about thirty other cons. An enormous man sits in a corner singing at the top of his voice. Nobody looks in a hurry to challenge him. He has just been to court to be sentenced. He got life.*

*'WB0874 McConnell?'*

*'Yes, Boss.'*

*'Here's your card. You're on C-wing. Move.'*

*We all wait nervously in line with our cutlery and cell cards. The screw unlocks the gate and the door behind it and we are ushered into the prison proper. There are cons everywhere. They're playing pool, playing cards, standing, sitting. But they all stop what they're doing and just stare in silence at us. One of them blows me a kiss. The tension is palpable. Some of the men in our group greet people they know, but for the most part we just stare at our feet and wait for the screw to lock the door behind us. We're desperately trying to appear invisible.*

Armley Prison was very different from the one at Horfield. Armley was an old diamond-shaped Victorian prison. Rumour had it that it used to be a brewery before someone had the smart idea of turning it into a prison. It looked like it hadn't been cleaned for a long time. It smelled like it hadn't been cleaned for a very long time.

The chief screws operated at the centre of the prison, and four wings (A, B, C and D) went off in different directions. There were two more wings, but they were off in a separate part of the building. A large steel gate sealed off each wing, and each wing had four landings with cells on either side. Cons, dressed in blue and grey or brown and grey, lived on each landing. The blue was for those already convicted of their crimes and the brown was for those on remand, those still awaiting sentence - or even the faint hope of getting a not guilty verdict.

The smell of urine, faeces and sweat was so overwhelming that I was gagging before I even got into my cell. The walls may once have been white but they were now yellow, covered in graffiti and smeared with all sorts of unmentionable stains. The whole room measured maybe twelve foot square, if that. There were two iron beds, a large jug, a table and chair and a bucket in the corner. The bucket was full to the brim and rested in a puddle of urine on the floor.

*'Welcome to your new home, Son.'*

*The steel door slams shut behind me and I sit on one of the beds. There's someone hidden under the bedclothes on the other bed. An old man peers out looking pretty scared.*

*'Alright, Mate?'*

*I nod.*

*'I'm only doing fourteen days for non payment of fines and I get out tomorrow.'*

*This bloke is so scared that he hasn't left the room in seven days. But when he sees that I'm not a mass murderer he visibly relaxes and begins to jabber away about his family and what he's going to do when he gets out.*

*I'm not really listening to him. How did I end up here? How did it come to this? What am I going to do now?*

*There's a noise of keys being jangled at the door. I'll become accustomed to that sound over the coming months. The cell door suddenly swings open.*

*'Association, lads.'*

*I walk out of my door and look around properly to try to get my bearings. Below me are the 'ones' and 'twos' and above me are the 'fours'. There are men everywhere, some emptying their buck-*

ets, some just chatting, smoking and doing their business. A queue quickly forms for the two telephones on the ground floor.

I take the opportunity to empty our bucket. Underneath me is a wire mesh that covers the two landings below us. It's apparently there to stop suicide attempts from the threes and fours. (I was later to find out that it was really to protect the screws from having things dropped on their heads from above). Some lads are at a table playing cards. Another queue is forming around a tired old pool table. The 6 o'clock news is on the television. Nothing much is happening so I go back to sit in my cell.

## From bad to worse

A scream rang out from below me and I rushed to the landing. A man was lying in a crumpled heap on the floor in front of the television. The back of his head was pouring with blood and his legs twitched violently. Another con, with a sock full of pool balls, stood over him and screamed obscenities in his direction. A whistle sounded, and within seconds he was buried underneath a pile of screws, pinned to the floor, cuffed and taken away. The twitching man was dragged off to the infirmary. Men on every landing kicked their doors and shouted and swore as they threw all sorts of junk on to the wire nets. Another whistle sounded and more screws suddenly appeared. I went back to my cell and closed the door.

'Oi! Your name Mez?'

I nod.

'From your kid, Son.'

My brother, who is doing a five stretch, has sent me half an ounce of tobacco, some cigarette papers, matches and a pile of old newspapers to read. I roll a fag, sit back and relax. Maybe it wasn't going to be so bad after all.

'Lights out!'

It starts off as a low grumble, then suddenly there's a wall of noise as men shout and scream to each other from across the different wings. Some are friends and others are swearing and making all sorts of threats. *Other men are swinging a 'line' across to each other. Usually it's a matchbox with a length of string attached to it that's swung out of one cell window to another. Inside can be tobacco, cannabis or even heroin. It requires great skill and patience, and it's the lifeline of the prison economy.*

*The nonces on B-Wing are really taking some stick. Nonces are rapists, perverts, paedophiles and grasses. They're the lowest of the low, the true scum of the prison world. Every prisoner lives with the dream of finding the Holy Grail - an unprotected nonce. They live in a high security part of the prison behind reinforced bars, in a prison within a prison. But sometimes they are sloppy and wander over into the general population. If discovered, they are made to regret It - painfully. To get a nonce is to be elevated to celebrity status.*

'Up! Slop out!'

*I take my bucket to one of the big sinks that are on the end of each landing and pour the contents into it. The stench from hundreds of such buckets is unbearable. In Bristol each cell has a toilet, but things seem much more primitive here.*

'Right, back in your cell!'

'Stand back! Stand back!'

*We stand back and watch as four screws knock a man to the floor. We are being transported to court and he wasn't too keen for the screws to check inside his backside. So they pin him to the floor. One kneels on his head, one on the base of his spine and one on his legs as the fourth one cuffs his hands behind his back. When they finish they boot him in the kidneys. I just keep my head down. It isn't my problem.*

'I think you're going to get at least two years.'

'You what? You're supposed to be my brief. Sort it out.'

'There's nothing I can do. Just hope that you get a good judge.'

*I sit back in the holding cell with about ten other men, all of us waiting to face the judge for sentencing. Every time a man comes back someone asks what he got. So far no one has got under four years, which means that the judge is a hard case. The guy before me gets life.*

*I'm escorted into the dock by a very large screw and I stand there while the two counsels argue it out, answering only to my name and the fact that I'm serving a sentence in Armley. I have absolutely no clue what's going on or what's being said. After about ten minutes I get nine months on top of my other six, giving me fifteen months in total. With good behaviour I'll only do about seven and a half months. What a result!*

### 'On the meat'

*'McConnell! On your feet!'*

*A screw dressed all in white suddenly appears at my cell. I get up and follow him as he escorts me off the wing. His keys rattle in the lock and the door swings open. I'm in a part of the prison that I've never seen before.*

*'Where're we going, Boss?'*

*'Kitchens, lad. You're starting there today.'*

*'Here he is Mr Curly, Sir. WB0874 McConnell.'*

*Mr Curly is the chief kitchen screw and he makes it plain that that is his name. He evidently doesn't like to be called 'Boss.' He is a big, gruff Scotsman who has clearly had some work done on his head. He has a scar that runs all the way around the hairline where some thatch work has gone wrong! I do my best not to stare at it.*

*'Pots and pans. Now.'*

The whole kitchen was run on a performance related scheme. The harder you worked, the quicker you were moved on to a better-paid job. Pots and pans, simply washing up duty, was the dirtiest and hardest job as well as being the lowest paid. We had to wash and clean everything in a prison of 1100 men who ate three times a day. I got stuck in, happy to be out of the soul-destroying cycle of being locked in my cell. My kitchen timetable was as follows:

0600 - Report to kitchen for work duty

0700 - Assigned a team to serve on the wing(s)

0800 - Back to kitchen for wash up, clean floors, sinks, ovens etc.

1200 - on wing(s) to serve lunch

1300 - Lunch
1330 - Lock up
1500 - back to kitchen for wash up
1600 - Serving tea on wing(s)
1700 - Wash up
1800 – Finish and go back to own wing
1800 - 2000 - association
2000-0600 - lock up

We worked a seven day week, twelve hours a day for a wage (on wash up duties) of about £5. The highest pay was over £10 for a team leader or a red band. A red band is a trustee of the prison and could walk around more or less unaccompanied. Although the work was hard it did make the time go by more quickly. There was only one part of the job that I didn't like. In fact, it was hated by every con in the kitchens, serving on the wings.

*'You! What's your name?'*

*'McConnell.'*

*'First name, Son?'*

*'Mez'*

*'Right, I'm John, and this is my serving team. You're coming out with us for breakfast.'*

*We wheel our hotplate through the prison wings until we arrive on C-wing where we lift the lids and set out the tables. Each man is given a serving spoon, or some plastic gloves if he's dishing out toast.*

*'Right, Mez, you're new so you're on the bacon. They get one piece only. OK?'*

*'Yeh, whatever.'*

*'OK boss. Let them out.'*

*The screws let the cons out one landing at a time. Each one comes, collects a metal tray and then walks down the serving line to get his food, fill his cup with hot water at the urn before going back to his cell.*

*'I want another bit.'*

*'You what?'*

58

'You heard me. I want another bit of bacon.'

The guy is enormous and mean looking. In fact, looking down the queue, they're all mean looking. I shrug and give him another piece. My first mistake.

'I want another bit as well.'

'You can't have one, Mate. I'm only allowed to give you one piece.'

'You gave him another piece. If you don't give me another piece I'm gonna rip your head off.'

I look down the line at my serving team for some help but they're all just keeping their heads down. I look at our kitchen screw for some guidance. He just smiles smugly at me. I give him another piece. I feel a tap on my shoulder. It's the kitchen screw.

'Only one piece each, McConnell.'

'But he was gonna rip my head off, Boss.'

A shrug. 'If you run out of bacon, there's going to be a riot. Do you understand?'

'Yes, boss.'

I suddenly realise why I've been put 'on the meat,' as it was known. The kitchen screws order us to ration the food out equally in order to feed the 300+ men on the wing. If we run out then there is no more. So, in order to ensure that everybody gets some, we can only give out one piece at a time. The problem, as I have just discovered, is that grown men want more than one rasher of greasy bacon. They want two or three. Most of them know the score and are cool about it, but there are plenty of muppets who just want to be right pains. That's when the real trouble starts. And it starts every mealtime without fail.

'I want more toast.'

'You can't have any. One piece each.'

'Give me another piece or I swear I'll do you.'

'Yeh, whatever. Just take one, Mate, alright?'

I pushed the hotplate back towards the kitchens so I didn't see him jump out behind me and smack me on the head with his metal tray. By the time I get off the floor he has been beaten into a bloody pulp by the rest of my team. Suddenly there are screws everywhere and he's taken off to solitary while I go to the doctor.

*'Oi, Mate. You serving on D-wing tonight?'*
*'Yeh.'*
*'Will you give this to Johnno for me?'*
*It's a little plastic envelope full of smack. Everyone knows Johnno. He's doing life for killing his wife's boyfriend. I pass it on and make two new friends. That's the way it works. I could charge, but I decide that I need friends more than I need snout. That's how it goes. Tobacco, letters, phone cards, drugs, they all get passed on from wing to wing. A favour here, a favour there. Building up friends in case of emergency.*

Cons came and went, and our team was chopped and changed almost every week. Somebody either was released or busted and a replacement came in. The new blood always went straight on the meat, which meant promotion for the rest of us. After the meat came the spuds, which sometimes caused hassle, but not very often. Then came the vegetables, nobody asks for more of them. The plum job was the butter at the end of the queue. You could give as much of that away as you liked. It was a sweet job and stress free.

## A prize scalp

*'You see this guy coming? Give him the smallest portion of everything that you can get away with.'*
*'Why, who is he?'*
*'Nonce.'*
*'What did he do?'*
*'Him and his friends gang raped two school girls.'*

The nonce was let out of his cell by himself and usually before all the other cons. He was known as a 'Cat A' prisoner and had bright yellow stripes running down the side of his clothes. The stripes were there to mark him out clearly in the event of a riot and/or escape. Those dressed in stripes were marked men, the highest risk prisoners in the system. He was always accompanied to the hotplate by two screws, one on either side. This nonce strutted along, grinning from ear to ear. Somebody spat on some potatoes and then handed them to him. We gave him the smallest and scabbiest portions we could find. He knew the score and just kept on smiling, taunting us. His would be a prize scalp to claim. His time would come.

*'I want more.'*

*'Nonces don't get more.'*

*'Give me more or I'm going to kill you.'*

*The team stop and wait. We look to the screws guarding him. They take a step backwards and then walk to the other end of the wing. All ten of us are up and over the tables beating him into a bloody pulp with fish slices, metal trays and steel ladles. Suddenly, a whistle sounds and about twenty screws rush to the scene. We're back behind the serving area trying to look as innocent as possible.*

*'What happened here?'*

*'Dunno, boss. I think he slipped over.'*

*'Don't get clever, Son. What happened?'*

*'Didn't see a thing, Boss.'*

He was taken to hospital and we never saw him again. We heard he'd been ghosted (moved) to another nick for his own protection. That's what you got if you were a nonce. The courts handed out sentences but we dealt in real justice.

*'Where's this hotplate going?'*

*'A-wing. Rule 43s.'*

*'Nonces?'*

*'Yeh.'*

*'Well, let's add a little extra spice to their food.'*

A little extra spice could be anything from crushed glass or cock-roaches to urine.

*'He's in the shower now - all by himself. If you're going to do it, then do it now.'*

*'What do I do?'*

*'Just fill your mug with hot water and sugar and make sure you get him in the face. It works just like acid. Sticks to them like glue.'*

*'Quick, before a screw comes!'*

*One by one we pour our slop buckets under the gap of the cell door. There are about a dozen buckets in all.*

*'Who's this one?'*

*'A priest, I think. He nonced a nine month old baby.'*

*Another nonce got it this morning. Someone stabbed him in the buttocks. Apparently he squealed like a baby.*

*Why do I do these things? Where's the justice in this world? How can one man get nine months for noncing a kid and another get three years for stealing a car? Sort that one out, God.*

Sometimes I think about God and all that stuff when I'm alone in my cell, but the noise of life just seems to block it all out.

*Some lad got raped today on B-wing. He was a first timer like me. We were on total shut-down until the busies arrived and sorted it out. Freaks me out thinking about it. It could happen to anyone.*

*'Here's your eggs. That's one phone card. OK?'*

*'Yeh. Can you wait till pay day?'*

*'Yeh.'*

Smuggling the stuff out was easy: eggs, bacon, bread and tea bags. Fruit was the favourite because it was good for making hooch. I could get anything you wanted in exchange for tobacco, phone cards or drugs. I even accepted the odd watch or jewellery.

*'Got any burn, Mez?'*

*'Yeh. How much do you want?'*

*'Half ounce?'*

*'Yeh. Three quarters back though. OK?'*

*'Yeh.'*

And so it went on. Drugs, phone cards and tobacco. Whatever you borrowed was paid back with interest. Sometimes I gave the odd freebie just to keep some friends in the right places. Nobody could ever pay back their debt fully, which meant that I had an endless supply of tobacco and phone cards coming in every week. It wasn't much, but it kept me going.

The balloons containing the weed (marijuana) had to be the right size; not too big and not too small, otherwise you could choke to death on them. We had our ways of getting them in. Seven or eight balloons were usually enough. Getting them out was the tricky part. For that I had to wait for twenty four hours to let nature take its course. Once they were out, I cleaned them up and we were in business. Easy.

*We've got some new blood for the team, an Asian fella in for drugs.*

'You. New blood. You're on the meat.'

'No way. I'm not touching that meat. It's ham.'

'So? You're on the meat. No arguments!'

'But I'm a Muslim!'

'Tell that to the kids you got hooked on smack, muppet! There're no Muslims, Jews or Christians in here, mate. No God, just cons. You're on the meat. Now!'

'Boss! This guy is being racist. He's making me serve the ham.'

*Big mistake. Massive mistake.*

In a mysterious turn of events a young Muslim convict was found beaten unconscious in his cell. It appears he slipped over and banged his head several times against the metal frame of his bed.

# 8

# 250 MILES FOR 15 MINUTES

*I got a letter this morning from one of those Christians. They want to know if they can come and see me. Why not? I don't get that many visitors anyway. Maybe they'll be good for a bit of snout. I decide to send them a Visiting Order.*

*I got another letter this morning from a girl called Paula. She reckons she wants to be my friend. She got my address from these Christians and decided to write to me. A bit weird, if you ask me. Maybe this is how they get you? They get a girl to play with your head and then they suck you into their little group. I'm going to have to watch this lot. You don't just start writing to people to be their mate. It just doesn't happen. People only want to be your friend if you've got something, especially if it's drugs. But this lot aren't into any of that. So what do they want then? I wonder if they get money for each person they 'convert'? There's got to be some blag going on here.*

*'How are you, Mez?'*
   *'Alright, thanks.'*
   *'You don't look too good.'*
   *'You know how it is. Life's tough.'*

They came. These people travelled 250 miles to visit me for fifteen minutes. They even brought me a personal stereo so that I could listen to music. I don't know who's more freaked out here, them or me?

> *'Right, time's up, McConnell.'*
> *'OK, Boss.'*
> *'Thanks for coming.'*

For the first time since I'd met these people they never once referred to Jesus or God. They talked to me like a real person and not some pet project. For the first time I began to take their message seriously. Maybe there was something to all this Jesus stuff after all. I mean, who would come all that way for a fifteen minute chat with a bloke who does nothing but give them grief? These guys must really be serious - or complete nutters.

> *'You just had a visit, Mez?'*
> *'Yeh.'*
> *'What'd you score?'*
> *'Nada. Nothing. Well, I got a stereo.'*
> *'Don't give me that. You must have scored something?'*
> *'I'm telling you, I didn't get a thing. They were Christians or something. They're not into all that.'*
> *'You what? Christians? What're Christians doing visiting you?'*
> *'I dunno. Met them on the outside just before I came in.'*
> *'You're not gonna become a Jesus freak are you, into God and all that?'*
> *'Yeh, right. What do you think? I'm just on my way to church now.'*

*I can't become a Jesus freak. I wouldn't last two minutes in here. Jesus is for gimps, lifers and old men who've lost their marbles. But what if it's true? What if it really is true?'*

> *'McConnell!'*
> *'Yes, Boss.'*
> *'Your application to go to the library has been approved.'*
> *'Nice one, Boss.'*
> *'I didn't even know you could read, McConnell.'*
> *'Careful, Boss. They could lock you up for being that funny.'*

I managed to find a book about some guy who had become a Christian while he was in prison. The book wasn't too big so I just stuffed it down the front of my pants and then picked up something by Stephen King. There was no way I was going to sign out some Christian book. As nobody else was going to read it, I figured that I might as well blag it.

*'Are you joking me or what? What's this old boy on? Apparently Jesus had visited him in his cell with two angels. According to this old con they had all appeared in pin stripe suits! What a wacko! He's been smoking too much weed.'*

*Throwing the book across my cell, I put thoughts of God to the back of my mind. Angels in pin stripe suits! I'm not having that!*

*'McConnell, you got your Cat D rating.'*

   *'What does that mean, Boss?'*

   *'It means you'll be doing your last three months at Lindholme in Doncaster. It's a nice little holiday camp, Son.'*

   *'Cheers, Boss.'*

We chopped mile after mile of cabbage for hours and hours every day. If we were lucky, sometimes we got to stand in the truck and sort out the good from the bad. But most days it was just chopping and picking until our backs ached. It was cold and it rained most of the time. I longed to return to Armley and the kitchens. Sometimes we'd read in the papers about how easy we had it in prison and we'd have a laugh together. Cutting cabbages eight hours a day for a fiver a week wasn't our idea of an easy life!

### Release

*'McConnell!'*

   *'Yes, Boss.'*

   *'Get yourself sorted, Son. You've had some days back from the police and you're on your way out tomorrow first thing.'*

   *'Nice one, Boss.'*

   *'Right, who wants my radio?'*

*'Me. Nice one, Mez.'*

*'Here's some burn, some cards and some gear. Enjoy.'*

*When I get out I'm going to sort myself out and get my head together. No more gear, no more blags. I'm going to get a job and be a proper person with a house and everything.*

*'Up already, McConnell.'*

*'Oh yes, Boss. I'm out of here today.'*

*'Off to processing first, Son.'*

*'Sign for your clothes.'*

*'Sign that you agree to the terms of your release.'*

*'Sign that this will be your address upon release.'*

*'If you break any of these terms you will be arrested immediately and returned to finish the duration of your sentence with the probability that you will receive a further term of imprisonment on top. Do you understand?'*

*'Sign here to affirm that during the period of your imprisonment you have had no cause for complaint against any warder or any other person employed by Her Majesty's Prison Services.'*

*'What if I don't?'*

*'Don't what?*

*'Agree with what you've said and to signing this thing?'*

*'Don't be an idiot, Son. If you don't sign then you don't get released. Simple as that. So just shut up and sign the forms.'*

*'Take this, McConnell.'*

*'What is it, boss?'*

*'It's a one way rail ticket courtesy of Her Majesty herself and a few quid spending money. Don't drink it all at once. Remember to report to your parole officer as soon as you get home or we'll be seeing you soon. Now, don't let me ever see your face again.'*

*'Don't worry, you won't.'*

The gates swung open and I stepped outside. I had stepped outside many times before on my way to the fields to work. But this time I was not under guard. This time I was a free man. I took a deep breath and waited for the feeling of elation I was told would come. I watched as wives, girlfriends, children and parents met those

released with me. But nobody came for me. I was a twenty-two--
year-old, drug addicted, ex con with thirty quid in his pocket and a
chip on each shoulder. A wave of anger and regret swept over me.
Prison had not changed me. I narrowed my eyes in determination
and headed for the nearest train station. Once again I found myself
alone.

# 9

# JESUS FREAK

Everybody thinks about the first thing they're going to do when they get out of prison. Some go straight to the pub, some score a bit of gear, some see their wives/girlfriends or both. Me? I went to the first bakery I could find and bought a giant chocolate éclair. Absolutely cracking!

*'Right, Mez, play by the rules and we'll get along fine. OK?'*

*'Yeh.'*

*'Right, I see you've got an address. My job as your probation officer is to ensure that it's suitable for you.'*

*'What do you mean, suitable?'*

*'I mean no dealers, for a start.'*

*'Yeh, right. The fella that lives there is one of those born again Christian types. He wouldn't know what gear was if you stuck it in his face.'*

*'Rules are rules. I'll be around in a couple of days. You better ring your friend so that he can come and pick you up. And try to keep your nose clean.'*

*'Hi Mez.'*

*'Alright, Matt?'*

*'Welcome to your new home.'*

It was a very nice little gaff. Certainly not what I'd been used to. It all looked so clean and fresh that I was practically afraid to touch anything in case I polluted it.

*'Listen, Mate, I appreciate this. Without you I wouldn't have got out. Nice one.'*

*'Well, God teaches us that we should look after those in need.'*

*'Don't be starting in with all that God stuff, Mate, all right? I'm not that grateful. I told you in my letter that I'm not interested in all that Jesus stuff. I don't want to hear it. OK?'*

*No more drugs and no more trouble. I'm gonna sort my life out.*

*'Hey Mez man, how's it going? When did you get out?'*

*'Two weeks ago.'*

*'You should have come to see me. We could smoke a bit of weed for old time's sake.'*

*'Nah. I'm not into that any more.'*

*'Yeh, right.'*

*'Serious. I'm trying to go straight and I am staying drug free.'*

*'Yeh, whatever. Where you living?*

*Man, that's just round the corner from me. Tell you what, come around tonight and we'll have a little party to celebrate.'*

*'Maybe.'*

*'Mez!'*

*'Mez! Good to see you, Mate!'*

*'Mez! Looking well, Mate.'*

*'Mez! Come in! Come in! Nice one, Mate, we knew you'd come. Just like old times, hey?'*

It came from nowhere: speed, Charlie, Es, and acid – all the old favourites. People were falling over themselves to give them to me. It would have been rude to turn them down.

*'Why not? Just for old time's sake, eh?'*

*I didn't go back to Matt's for three days.*

*I hate myself. I hate my life.*

*The panic attacks are back and worse than ever. I can't sleep. I'm going to die and nobody can do a thing about it. God help me! I can't eat. Somebody help me! I feel so alone.*

*'Got any gear?'*

*'Yeh, how much?'*

*'Just give us a couple of grams to get my head sorted.'*

*'You all right, Mez? You look wasted.'*

*'Man, my head's battered. I need to get away from my life, from my head. There's got to be more to it all than this, hasn't there?'*

*'More to what?'*

*Life, man. Life.'*

*'Man, you are trashed. Get it together, Mez.'*

*'What do you think happens when we die?'*

*'I don't know! Listen, Mate, that's a bit heavy, isn't it? Just chill out.'*

*'Don't you ever think about it? Life? What's it all about? What happens when we die? We're all going to die someday. What happens then? Where do we go? What will happen to us?'*

*'Did prison fry your head or what?'*

*Jesus Christ is the only way to God. God is holy. God is love. Repent of your sins. Put your trust in Jesus. They talk about it all the time but what does it mean? Life is just senseless. Why should it have a point anyway? God! God is for muppets who can't handle the truth. There's no one out there. No one loves us. We're on our own.*

*I saw them today, the Christians. They came round to Matt's house for dinner and they sat around the table holding hands and praying or something. I think it was praying. I've never seen anyone pray at a table before, except on 'Little house on the Prairie.' They all look so squeaky clean and perfect. Sometimes I want to believe what they say but then they go and do weird stuff like that. I mean, I don't want to be holding hands with another man and praying. How sick is that?*

*They seem happy, these Christians. Well, happier than anybody I've ever known. They all wear nice clothes and drive nice cars and invite each other to dinner. I suppose I'd be happy too if I'd a few* quid in my pocket. But I think it's more than that. There's something different about them and I can't quite work it out.

'Mez, have you repented of your sin and accepted the Lord Jesus Christ into your heart yet?'

'You what?'

*Some of these people are truly off their heads.*

'Have you accepted Jesus as Lord of your life?'

'You better get yourself out of my face. All right? Or you'll be accepting my fist as lord of your dentures. Know what I mean?'

*Lord of my life? What's all that about? How do you make some bloke you can't see Lord of your life? And what's all this 'accept him into your heart' lark. Sometimes they talk about blood and it freaks me out. I mean, is this some sort of weird cult or what? Man, my head is spinning. I need to get away. I need time to think. To clear my head.*

'Mez?'

'Matt?'

'Our church youth group is going on a weekend away to Wales and I just wondered if you fancied tagging along?'

'Yeh, nice one. You're not going to try and convert me though, are you?'

'No. It's just a weekend away where we learn stuff from the Bible.'

'OK. But keep your freaky mates away from me. I don't want to be hearing about any more of that blood of the Lamb stuff. All right?'

'Fair enough.'

'OK, let's all sing number 253!'

*I look around the room and there are about thirty young people aged between sixteen and twenty-five. Some of them look like class A gimps but most of them look normal. Then they all stand to sing this song about Jesus and love and all that. There they go mentioning the blood again. I mean, they even sing about this stuff! I feel like a bit of a div being the only one still sitting so I stand with my hands in my pockets staring at the floor.*

'OK. Let's turn to the Word of God. This weekend we're going to be studying the book of Ezra.'

*Ezra? Why don't these people have proper names like Dave or Rob or something? I need a fag.*

*They really get on together this lot, don't they? They seem to have something. I can't put my finger on it. But they seem to have this bond that I've never seen before. They might talk a load of nonsense but there's no denying that they've got something. And I can tell you, whatever it is I don't have it.*

'Hurry up or we'll be late for church!'

*I can't believe that I'm going to church. But as there's a big group of us, and I don't feel so conspicuous, I figure that I'll give it a go. See what all the fuss is about.*

'Good morning, brethren. If you are a visitor here, then we welcome you in the precious name of the Lord Jesus Christ.'

'Matt. What's a brethren?'

'It's like people. Good morning, everyone.'

'So why didn't he just say that then?'

'I don't know.'

'Let us pray. Oh Lord, we know that thou art our heavenly Father and that we are thy humble servants. We beseech thee in the Name of thy precious Son to hear our supplications this morning.'

'Matt. Why's he talking like that?'

'Shh. He's praying to God.'

'What? Does God understand him then? Do you all talk like that to God?'

'Let us stand and sing together hymn number 202.'

'Sit. Here are this week's notices.'

'Stand. Let us sing number 543.'

'Sit. Let us turn in our Bibles to the Acts of the Apostles.'

'Let us pray.'

'Let us stand and sing hymn number 21.'

*Some really old guy stands up and begins to talk about God and the Bible and sin and stuff.*

'Matt. Don't you get bored talking about the same stuff all the time?'

'We don't talk about the same stuff all the time.'

*'Yeh you do: sin and Jesus and hell and repentance and faith and all that.'*

*This guy talks for nearly an hour. Sometimes he shouts, sometimes he talks and sometimes he whispers. He's obviously very excited about whatever it is he's talking about.*

*'Let us stand and sing number 789.'*

*'So what did you think, Mez?'*

*'About what?'*

*'Church.'*

*'Is it like that every week?'*

*'More or less.'*

*'Then it's rubbish.'*

*'Why?'*

*'It was long and boring for a start. Half the time I didn't have a clue what that guy was saying up the front. And what's with all that standing and sitting. And how come you all know exactly when to do it? It was just too weird. Half the people in that place looked more miserable than some of my friends doing time in Armley.'*

*'Matt?'*

*'What?'*

*'If I became a Christian, would I have to learn to pray like that bloke from the church?'*

*'No. We all pray in our own way.'*

*'So there's not like a special way to pray and stuff?'*

*'No, why? Are you interested?'*

*'No! Just asking.'*

*Sometimes I can't sleep at night just thinking about God and the Bible. Sometimes I get this overwhelming urge to pray, but I just can't. I feel stupid just entertaining the thoughts. Yet, no matter how hard I try, I can't seem to get God out of my mind. In a desperate attempt to sort my head out I've decided that I'm not going to go to church again. If I don't go to church then surely they can't play with my head.*

I found a Bible today in Matt's house. It was just lying there on the table so I took a quick look. I read some stuff but it didn't make any sense. Next to it there was a big book called Matthew Henry's Commentary on the Bible. It had bits of the Bible in it and then a bit of an explanation. I started at Genesis and began to read.

*I don't want to hang out with my mates anymore. It's weird. I'm well into this Matthew Henry bloke's book, and I'd rather stay in and read that. I haven't told Matt that I'm reading it because I'd feel a bit stupid.*

*How can I be a sinner? I didn't ask for my life. It was given to me. If there are any sinners, they're the people who brought me up. They made me what I am. It's not my fault. My social worker told me that I was just a product of my environment. She said that if I'd come from a good home, I would never have got into trouble. But this Paul bloke is saying that we're all sinners. He's saying that none of us has any excuse. I'm not having that. I bet this Paul bloke didn't get a good kicking when he was growing up.*

*How can we trust someone we can't see? I mean, where's the proof that we're not talking to ourselves?*

*The Bible says that there's only one way to God and that's through faith in Jesus Christ. It says that there's no other way to be saved from hell. That can't be true, can it? I mean, what about the other religions? Are you telling me that all those people are liars and deluded? This Bible is a bit harsh.*

*I think I might be a sinner, you know. I mean, I've done some terrible stuff in my life. And if God sees everything, then how can he forgive me for some of the stuff that I've done?*

*'Matt, if you become a Christian does God forgive you for everything you've ever done?'*

*'Yes. The Bible says that once we become Christians he remembers our sins no more.'*

*'But that's too easy. How does he know that people don't just become Christians to feel better about themselves?'*

*'God knows our hearts.'*

*'You what?'*

*'God knows our deepest thoughts and motives.'*

> '*OK.*'
> '*Why, are you beginning to think about the gospel?*'
> '*Nah, not really.*'

*Apparently this Jesus bloke was the only person in history to be completely perfect - sinless. The Bible says that when he went to the cross he took the sins of his people upon himself. I'm not too sure what that means. I think it's got something to do with this blood they're always going on about.*

*I wonder if I have to wear a tie and get a centre parting if I become a Christian?*

*I woke up tonight thinking about Jesus. If what the Bible says is true, then Jesus was innocent and yet he willingly chose to go to the cross in the place of guilty people. I mean, what was that all about? Nobody does stuff for other people without some hidden agenda, right? If God loved him, then why did he let Jesus do that? It just doesn't add up at the minute. If my old man gave me up to die, I don't think we'd be staying the best of mates!*

> '*Mez, have you thought any more about eternity, about the gospel?*'
> '*Nah.*'
> '*Why not?*'
> '*It does my head in.*'

*I can't sleep. I can't think. I can't even have a fag in peace. I just feel hyper all the time. Jittery. Nervous. I don't know what I feel anymore. I just can't seem to focus on anything other than Jesus. He's just in my head constantly, mocking me with his sinlessness and his death and resurrection. I need to go for a walk.*

*I had to talk to God today. I didn't want to, but I just knew that if I didn't then I'd explode. I told him that I couldn't believe in him. I mean, how could I? How could I be sure I wasn't just talking to myself? I told him to leave me alone and go and find someone else to bug with all this religious stuff.*

*'OK God. Here's the deal. I'll give up smoking and doing the drugs if you prove to me beyond all doubt that you exist. I can't say fairer than that, can I? Nice one.'*

I was sitting on a park bench when it happened. It was the 3rd of May 1995. I remembered that I hadn't had a fag for three days and my head was well and truly mashed. I just sat looking at a flower. A simple daisy it was. I suddenly realised that this flower didn't get here by accident. It wasn't the result of some cosmic explosion millions of years ago. It was created; it was quite clearly designed and perfect in every way. God was a reality that I had to face.

*Jesus has left me nowhere to run. I've been busted. I can't hide behind my background, my life and my childhood anymore. I can't excuse my behaviour, my feelings and my problems. I have to face the fact that I am a sinner. I have to take responsibility for my own actions. But I don't want to. Everything within me is trying to fight, to escape these truths. I feel like I'm drowning. I can't get my guilt out of my mind. But I'm scared that I'll have to give up all my hate when I want to keep it with me. I'm scared that I'll have to forgive those who don't deserve it. I'm scared that my life won't be my own anymore. I'm afraid of everything I'll have to give up. I want to be in control. In control! That's a joke! Is my life my own anyway? What would I have to give up? My misery, anguish, despair? I would be glad to get rid of them.*

*God is real. It's like the focus button has been turned inside my head and I can see the world clearly for the first time. God is real and I'm armpit deep in trouble! I've read about something called the Sinner's Prayer so I decide I'd better try and say that. The problem is that I've forgotten the words, so I just make up my own words and hope God won't mind too much if I don't stick to the usual formula.*

*'God. I'm a sinner. I've done some bad stuff in my life. Please forgive me. I want to put my trust in Jesus. I don't really understand very much, but I'm willing to give it a bash if you'll let me. Amen.'*

*Not a thing. Nada. Isn't something supposed to happen now? Where are all the singing angels, the blinding visions, the overwhelming emotional experiences? Maybe I haven't said the right prayer. I go back home to find the little booklet with the Sinner's Prayer at the back.*

*I can't sleep. I've done the Sinner's Prayer about ten times and still nothing's happened. Still no sign of those angels, no singing, not a dickey bird. What about that wonderful sense of peace I was supposed to have, the one that's supposed to surpass all understanding? I'm more stressed and worried now than I've ever been. What if God had changed his mind because I'd faffed about too much? It says in those testimony books that when you become a Christian you sleep really well at night. But I can't sleep! Does that mean I'm not a Christian then?*

*I said the Sinner's Prayer about a dozen times again today. I don't want to tell anyone about it because I would feel like a right muppet if I told people and then God didn't let me in the club.*

*This is getting out of hand. I've prayed about ten times today and yesterday and the day before that. I need to talk to someone who knows God a bit better than me, someone who's got one of those relationships they keep going on about.*

*'Dave?'*
   *'Yes.'*
   *'Could we meet up? I need to talk to you.'*
   *'I think I've become a Christian.'*
   *'You what?'*
   *'The thing is, I'm not too sure that God has heard me, if you know what I mean? I've prayed that Sinner's Prayer thing about fifty times and I haven't heard a thing from him. I just need to be sure, and I figured that, since you know him a bit better, you could ask him if it was OK. I'm not really one for all this praying and stuff. Maybe you could talk to God for me just to try and make sure.'*
   *Silence.*

We sat in a car in some back lane in Swindon and Dave prayed to God that he would help me in my faith and also that I had truly repented. When he finished, I prayed again and just said that I agreed with everything Dave had said. I apologised for being a bad person yet again just to make sure that God knew I was serious. Again nothing. Maybe I was just too bad to become a Christian? Dave assured me that everything was OK and that I was a Christian if I truly meant what I'd said to God.

*'You sure it's OK to pray in a car, Dave? I mean, I never heard of people praying in cars before.'*

*'It's fine, Mez. If you're a Christian, you have access to God twenty four hours a day, and you can reach him anywhere.'*

*'Man, how mad is that?'*

*'But what about the peace, Dave?'*

*'What peace?'*

*'The one that passes all understanding. I can't sleep at night so maybe God hasn't accepted me yet. Maybe I'm on the waiting list or something.'*

*'Mez, if you have truly repented of your sins and put your faith and trust in Jesus, then you have made your peace with God. It doesn't make any difference whether you sleep well or not.'*

*'Serious? Nice one! How about one last prayer, Dave, just to make sure?'*

**10**

# NEW LIFE

'*C*ongratulations, Mez. I understand that Jesus has become a re-ality in your life.'
'You what?'
'I understand that you've accepted the Lord into your heart.'
'You what?'
'You've become a Christian.'
'Oh yeh. Nice one, eh?'

I realised today that, for the first time in years, I don't feel black inside anymore. I actually feel quite hopeful, purposeful even. For the first time in my life I actually feel at peace with the world.

Church still freaks me out. Half the time I don't know what's being said, and those songs they sing! Some of the words are just beyond me. Man, what are this lot on! I feel like I'm going to a funeral every week. I thought we were meant to be going to the good place?

'What're you up to, Mez?'
'You what?'
'What's your game? What are you doing here?'
'I'm a Christian now, so why shouldn't I be in church?'
'You're a Christian! Right, whatever you say. Your type doesn't belong here. You're obviously up to something.'
'What're you saying, muppet? You saying I'm not a Christian? What's your problem?'

*I thought that all these people were supposed to be Christians? Apparently some of them think I'm in the game for ulterior motives. What, exactly? To win hip new mates and look cool in front of my old ones? What's going on? Why are they saying that I'm blagging?*

'Don't worry about it, Mez.'

'But they're not saying it about you, Matt.'

'Listen, you answer to God not to them. God knows what's going on inside you.'

'Yeh, well they can stuff their Christianity. I'm not going back to that church again.'

'It's just a couple of people. Everybody else is behind you.'

*I've started meeting up with this bloke from the church. His name is Mark and he knows everything about the Bible. It's called a discipleship class. Haven't got a clue what a disciple is? It's just another one of those freaky words they seem to use? I think this lot speak some sort of secret language that nobody else understands. I tell you what, they ought to give you a dictionary of freaky sayings when you become a Christian.*

*Man, I love my discipleship class. I get to learn about God and how he created the world and everybody in it, and I also get to ask every question I can think of. It's much better than that church lark. You're not allowed to ask questions there. You've just got to sit while some bloke goes on for forty minutes. I'm lucky if I understand ten minutes of it.*

*I've been clean for two months. Two months! I can't believe it. What's even freakier is that I don't even want to score or have a fag. I feel like I could take on the world.*

## Home ... too soon

'Are you sure it's a good idea, Mez?'

'Yeh, why not? It would give me a chance to sort out some unfinished business with people and a chance to talk to my family.'

'Yes, but you're still a very new Christian. You need to take things slowly.'

'I'll be alright, Matt.'

*I'm feeling a little nervous. I haven't been home for years. What am I going to say? By the way, I'm into God and that now? Jesus loves you? Are you covered by the blood of the Lamb? I haven't a clue what I'm going to say.*

'Long time no see. What're you doing back here?'

'Just thought I'd come for a quick visit.'

'Nice one. Some of us are going out for a drink later. Do you fancy one for old time's sake?

'Yeh, why not?'

*It is 3 am. The music is pounding and my head is spinning. What am I doing? One drink turned into eight or nine. The problem is that I feel really guilty. Christians shouldn't get drunk, should they? I dunno. I mean, I'm only having a good time after all. A little drink never hurt anybody, did it? So why do I feel so bad? I've never felt like this before? It's a bit weird really. I've got to pull myself together. It's only a beer.*

'What're you looking at?'

'Nothing, Mate.'

'Yeh, you are. You're looking at my missus, aren't ya?'

'Don't think so, Mate.'

'Yeh ya are. Fancy her, do ya?'

'No, I don't. Just go home, Mate. You've had too much to drink.'

*Why doesn't he just go home? But no, he has to push it and push it and now look at him. The whole side of his head is mashed in and there's blood everywhere. It's all over my new shirt, all over me.*

*I'm supposed to be telling them about my new life in Jesus, yet look at me. Drunk and fighting. My head is done in with Christian stuff. What am I supposed to do? I've got to watch my brother's back. That's the way it is. I know it's wrong. I know that violence isn't the way forward. I know that God doesn't want me to get into trouble, yet I don't want to let my family down. But I don't want to let God down either. I feel like I'm losing it. I feel so alone.*

'I'll be back in a minute.'

*I sit in the car and wait. Ten minutes later the back door opens and in comes a laptop computer, a video and a television.*

*'What you doing? You said this was your mate's place.'*
*'I lied. What's your problem? We've done this a hundred times.'*
*'Yeh, but I'm not into this any more.'*
*'Who are you trying to kid? Don't be a muppet.'*

I've been home for twenty four hours and I've already been drunk, had a fight and been an accessory to burglary. God must be tripping with me.

*People like me don't become Christians. What do I think I'm doing? I don't belong in church. I feel like I'm a schizophrenic. One part of my life is this and the other is singing hymns and going to Bible studies. How mad is that? I feel like I don't belong anywhere anymore.*

*My old stomping ground. Look at it. I've spent most of my life in this place and I didn't realise just what a dump it is. When I lived here it was home. It was all I knew. It was my entire world. It shaped my whole outlook on life. When I lived here everybody did drugs. Everybody was involved in one scam or another. But now I'm seeing the place with new eyes. Burned out cars, babies playing barefoot in glass-covered streets, smack-heads scoring on street corners, glue bags in front gardens, used needles in the gutters. I've grown up with it all my life, so why am I only seeing it now for the first time? Why do I feel so upset? This is life. What's happening to me? What am I supposed to do about it?*

*'Mez! I heard you were back. How's it going?'*
*'OK. You?'*
*'Oh, you know. Same old, same old thing.'*

That was the problem. I did know. In all the years since I'd been away nothing had changed. The same people were living the same lives in the same tired, predictable way. Nothing had moved forward. It was as though they were caught in some type of endless time warp, destined to live out their miserable lives trapped in this place.

Tears welled up inside me. I just wanted to hug my friend and tell him about Jesus and his great love for him. But I didn't cry, I didn't hug him and I didn't tell him about Jesus. We talked about nothing for a long time: the price of cigarettes, the local football team. His eyes were blank and he looked old before his time. He was trapped and he couldn't escape his life.

What was there for me if I gave up God? Nothing. I couldn't go back to that life again. I couldn't live like that anymore. My faith was all there was between me and a life of meaningless, hopeless desperation, moving from one con to the next. I had to get out of there. I was never going to give Jesus up. Never. Maybe I was a Jesus freak but that was better than the alternative. Anything was better than an excuse for a life.

*'Oh God, forgive me for my sins. Forgive me, forgive me, forgive me. Help me to sort my head out.'*

*'Oh God, why can't they see? Why can't they see the hopelessness of their lives? Why can't they see what I see?'*

*Am I going mad?*

*Now I'm angry. I'm angry at myself for messing up and I'm angry at my friends because they can't, they won't, see the truth. They'd rather bury their heads in the sand than admit that there's something wrong with their lives. I want to make them see, to force them. But I can't. I just can't. What am I going to do now?*

# 11

# **FINDING MY FEET**

'*So, Mr McConnell. Do you feel you have what it takes to become a member of our night staff?'*

'*Yes, I do.'*

'*It's hard work replenishing stock, but it can be rewarding work as well. Now, just one more thing before we conclude. It says here that you've been convicted of a criminal offence. Could you possibly expand upon that for me?'*

'*Yes. I've recently been released from prison and I've a criminal record dating back ten years.'*

'*I see.'*

'*But I'm a Christian now, so everything is sweet. You can sleep easy. I'm not going to rip off your store or anything.'*

'*A Christian? I see. Interesting. Well, we'll be in touch.'*

*I might as well have said 'alien' for all the good it did me.*

*I've got a job with an agency. I'm picking orders in a warehouse. Basically, I travel around on a little machine and pick stuff off shelves, load them on to pallets and dump them in loading bays for lorries to distribute them to stores around the country. It's not rocket science, but it's a job.*

*I've been here a week and my head is done in already. I can't do this. The same mind-blowing, boring stuff day in, day out. How can people live like this? How can they get up every day of their lives and* not question the point of it all? I feel like the life is being sucked right out of me.

My mates want me to score some gear and have a session with them, but I just can't. The problem is that I've got all this spare cash because I've cut out all the smoking and stuff. I've got nothing to spend it on really. I mean, what am I supposed to do with this money? It seems a shame to let it go to waste when I could be buying some gear to sell. But I just can't do that anymore. I'm a different person now. I'm following Jesus, so I've got to keep my head down and my nose clean.

Sometimes, when I'm alone at night, the voices come. One tells me that I should just get up and get out of here, and the other tells me to keep going. Sometimes I just get this urge to run and run and run. But the problem is that I've got nowhere to run to, and I'm not sure what I'm running from.

Every day I learn something new about Jesus Christ, and every day I have to face up to the truth about my sinful life. It was easier on the streets. No hassles, no responsibilities, no guilt. This Christian stuff is harder than I thought.

I've got myself a voluntary job with something called The Breakfast Club, a project that helps young homeless people. Should keep me out of trouble and maybe I'll get to tell some people about Jesus. About forty or fifty of them come every morning.

Some of these guys are blatant scroungers and the rest are just miserable looking, scruffy, abused drug addicts. Is that how I used to look? I come every day now and help to make the tea and serve the breakfasts. Some of them can't see past their next score. Their whole mind is just focused on getting enough money together to get through the day. And they say that I'm sad for being a Christian!

I've decided that I want to get baptised and tell people about what Christ has done for me.

I've enrolled at college. I want to do something more with my life. I'm not sure what, but I know I don't want to be working in warehouses and bumming around for the rest of my life. I'm taking some GCSEs and something called an access course in politics and history. It's only part time, but it means that I'm free to help at The Breakfast Club most mornings. I feel that my life has got some direction.

I've seen some of the volunteers dealing at The Breakfast Club. I shouldn't be shocked, but I am. Well, not shocked, more like disappointed. People just seem to come along, eat a hot meal, score some gear and go on their way. If anything, we seem to be making the situation worse not better. Why don't these Christians do something about it?

*It's my baptismal service today and I'm, well, nervous. I've never been up the front in a church before. Apparently I've to give something called a testimony, which is Christian-speak for telling people about what Christ has done for me on the cross. Some of the others talk about having 'a personal relationship with Jesus,' but I haven't a clue what they're on about. All I know is that Jesus died for my sins, I repented, he binned them all, and now I want to live according to his Word in the Bible. I'm not sure about all this 'personal relationship' stuff though. It's not like we meet up for coffee every week or anything.*

'Mark, don't you think that Christians ought to be doing something about the homeless problem in our area?'

'I do, Mez. What have you in mind?'

'Well, what about opening the church for a few days over Christmas. People could come and have something to eat and we could tell them about Jesus and stuff.'

'Sounds like a great idea. Go for it.'

'What do you mean you want to open the church for the homeless at Christmas?'

'I mean I want to open the church for the homeless at Christmas.'

'What do you want to do that for?'

'Because they're homeless and it's Christmas.'

'Well, I think it's a bad idea.'

'Why?'

'Because we don't want that type of person in our church.'

'Why not?'

'Listen, it will never get past the deacons.'

'What's a deacon?'

*The church has voted to open their doors for Christmas. I am well buzzing! Some people are still giving me grief, but stuff them. We're going to open up on Christmas Eve and stay open until the day after Boxing Day. I feel like I'm actually doing something for God, something that matters anyway.*

*Christmas was quality. About twenty young people came to stay with us over the three days, and sixty people from the church volunteered to come and do a shift at the church. The church donated piles and piles of clothes and loads of food. This lot may not have a clue about what's going on in the world, but they don't waste any time when it comes to getting stuck in! Maybe the church isn't full of muppets after all.*

## A New Direction

*'Edinburgh City Mission? What do you want to go to Edinburgh City Mission for?'*

*'It's only for eight weeks in the summer and then I'll come back and finish my course.'*

*'But you've only been a Christian for a few months!'*

*'So what? I just want to see how things are done by a proper mission. I just feel that maybe I could be useful for God somehow.'*

*'Man, this place is a dump!'*

*'Well, it's going to be your home for the next eight weeks.'*

*I'm living in a flat in the middle of an estate called Pilton in Edinburgh. What an absolute dive! It reminds me of home: burnt-out cars and houses, high-rise flats, used needles and glue bags in the gutters and kids just aimlessly wandering the streets.*

*'Keep your door locked at night, Son. It can get a bit rough. Any trouble, ring the police. You should be OK though. We've reinforced the door with steel and we've put bars on the windows because they just kept bricking them. Any questions?'*

*'Yeh. When do I start work?'*

*'Haven't a clue, Son. I'm just here to settle you in. Somebody from the Mission will call round and sort you out later.'*

*Nobody came.*

*I can hear people outside my window - laughing, joking, urinating, and vomiting. All the things you would expect on a Friday night. Every little noise makes me nervous. I'm so wired that I can't get to sleep. I turn the television on for a bit of company and soon drift off.*

*I get up early and go to the shops to buy some food because there's nothing in the flat. Going early always pays off because there's never anybody up. They're all crashed out, sleeping off the effects of the night before. That means little or no chance of trouble for a strange face on the estate. In my day a welcoming committee usually visited strange faces but, thankfully, all is quiet. I spend the day watching the television and waiting for someone to come, but nobody does. What sort of mission is this?*

*Sometimes the voices come again. What are you doing here? Just go home and stop being stupid. The Mission doesn't really want you here. If they did, they would've come to see you by now. Just go home. You're wasting your time. You're not really a Christian. Christianity is for good people, for nice people, not for people like you. Stop pretending. This is just an absolute joke. Get yourself out there, score some gear, have a smoke and forget about all this Christian rubbish. Who's gonna know if you score a bit of gear?*

*Bog off Satan. Get out of my head!*

*I need to find a church so I can get my head together. This looks like a decent enough place. I'll give this one a go. Man, this is like entering the twilight zone. Do these people know that there's a battleground outside their door? I feel a bit out of place now surrounded by all these posh people in their Sunday best. I'll give it a go though. It's got to be better than sitting in that flat by myself.*

*Right, there's a fella coming this way. By the looks of him I'd say he's the pastor. I've figured out that the normal people come in the back door but these pastor-type blokes have got their own door at the front. I wonder what they do in there? I wonder if they talk about the footie? This guy has got to be the pastor because he's shaking everybody's hand and patting people and all that. I'll say 'hello' when he comes my way.*

*Man, he's walking straight past me. Maybe he can't see me? Course he can! There are only a dozen people here! What, am I not good enough for his poxy church? Stuff this lot; they can stick their church. I'm off! I feel alone. I thought you were supposed to be with me all the time, God? Where are you? You're not here. It's all a big lie. Those Christians have been blagging you. It's all in their imagination. There is no God. Get real! If God is so real, why didn't that pastor come and say 'hello.' Christians are supposed to be nice to each other and help each other.*

*I'm scared now. What if it isn't real? What if it's all in my head? Where does that leave me? Maybe I should just jack this Christian lark in? They don't treat people very nicely, do they? At least my non-Christian mates are always glad to see me. I could just disappear from here and I'd never have to see these people again.*

*Just stay and think things through. Don't do anything rash.*

*Sometimes I have this overwhelming urge to just top myself, end it all, just to stop this battle within me. I'm really losing my marbles. One voice in my head's telling me one thing and another one's telling me something else.*

*'If you leave, where are you going to go? What are you going to do?'*

*'I dunno. But I'd survive. I always have.'*

*'What about your Christian friends?'*

*'What about them? Where are they now? If they were my mates, why haven't they rung me to see how I am? They're not interested now I've been converted.'*

*'What about God? He's interested in you. What about Jesus? He died for you.'*

*'I know, I know. It always comes down to him. But if I went back to the streets at least I wouldn't have to worry about this stuff all the time. At least I wouldn't have voices in my head telling me what I should and shouldn't do. Man, this Christian stuff is hard.'*

*My faith in Jesus is all I have left. My whole life hangs on my faith in him. Without him life is meaningless, pointless. Without him what am I? Without him where am I heading?*

## God speaks

*I put on a tape of Christian music to try and calm my mind, and I begin to read from a little booklet called 'Daily readings' that a friend gave me. The reading is Deuteronomy 31. Deuteronomy? Where's that? I look it up in the index and find it in the Old Testament. I read, 'The Lord himself goes before you and will be with you; he will never leave you nor forsake you. Do not be afraid; do not be discouraged' (Deuteronomy 31:8).*

*I feel goose bumps rising on my arms as I read the words. The pastor had told me that when we read the Word of God we literally are reading God's actual words, not words written by men about God, but written by men inspired by the Holy Spirit of God. Is God speaking to me? Nah, it has to be a coincidence. But I did just pray for God to help me, so why shouldn't he? Man, how freaky is this! God is speaking to me through the Bible! Everything is going to be OK if I just keep going on with him. Well, stuff Satan. He can do one!*

*All of a sudden I feel at peace. The doubts have gone. The fear has gone. I write out the words on a piece of paper and put it in my pocket so that I can memorise it.*

*'Nice one, God. Thanks for listening, and thanks for answering my prayers. Please help me to get through my time here and keep Satan off my case please. Amen.'*

A guy called Bill came to see me today and took me to the Headquarters of Edinburgh City Mission. I'm going to be spending most of my time with a girl called Rose who works for them full-time. She generally works alone and wanders the streets of Edinburgh with a rucksack full of sandwiches, a flask of tea and some Christian leaflets. Apparently there was a bit of an administrative mix up and nobody knew I was here. But this Bill is a nice bloke and was very apologetic.

The Mission also has a drop-in centre that opens two mornings a week. People come in for a warm drink, a sandwich and some clean clothes. It's quite different from The Breakfast Club because this place is staffed completely by Christians and we can talk openly about the Lord Jesus Christ to everyone and anyone who comes in.

Two hundred people came in today. Old, young, black and white. They queued around the street to get in. They all look so sad, so weary, so defeated by life. I wonder how God feels when he sees people suffering like this? I wonder if this is where God wants me to spend my life - helping the poor and destitute. I wonder if they realise just how much God loves them. I wonder how I can help them to understand the gospel without freaking them out.

'Would you like a drop of tea and a sandwich?'

They always do. Sometimes we tramp around the streets for hours without seeing anybody. Sometimes we can't get a hundred yards down the street before all our food and drink runs out. There's a lot of suffering out there, a lot of very lonely people. We found a couple unconscious on a park bench this morning. Both of them were so high that they hadn't even taken the needles out of their arms, and they were bleeding all over each other. We left them some food and a leaflet telling them about the love of Jesus. What else could we do?

*'We're going out with the Care Van tonight.'*

*'What's the Care Van?'*

*'It's a bus that has been converted so that we can serve hot drinks and sandwiches, hand out blankets, give information about hostels and talk about the Lord Jesus Christ.'*

*'Who drives it?'*

*'It's driven by lots of different people. In fact, we have volunteers from over forty churches. And the churches take it in turns to send people to go out with the van every night.'*

*'Fair play.'*

*'How old are you boys?'*

*'Thirteen.'*

*What're you doing here? Haven't you got somewhere to go?'*

*'No.'*

*'So where do you crash out?'*

*'In a skip down the road.'*

'How old are you, Mate?'
    '79 years old, Son.'
    'What're you doing on the streets at your age?'
    'Ach, well, I've been on the run from the CIA for the last twenty three years.'

There were many more. Each of them had a sad story to tell. Each was battered by life. All of them were trying to convince themselves that their life wasn't so bad and that somehow, some day, it would magically get better and it would all turn out alright in the end. Defiant, aggressive, hopelessly lost. Giving them soup and blankets just didn't seem like it was enough.

*I want to dedicate my life to serving God. I know deep down that I'll never work in a factory again. I'm going to be an evangelist working on the streets. No doubt about it. I can never go back to that life again. Ever.*

*I've been back in Swindon for two weeks and I'm still buzzing from my Scottish experience. I've been talking to a girl about Jesus and the Bible and she seems to be interested. The problem is that I don't know very much more than that Jesus died for our sins and we need to put our faith and trust in him. I'm reading the Bible a lot, but I'm not sure how much of it I really understand. I mean, I read a bit in it the other day about not moving your neighbour's boundary stone. When I asked someone in church what it meant, he just told me to let the Holy Spirit lead and guide me. What's all that about? And who's the Holy Spirit? That sounds a bit freaky. He said that we don't need to understand everything in order to have faith. Well, he might not, but I need to. I want to understand everything. I've got a million questions swimming around in my brain twenty four hours a day.*

## Scene: a graveyard near Swindon town centre
## Occasion: first evangelistic endeavour

'Look, you need to put your faith and trust in Jesus NOW – today.'
    'I'll do it when I get home.'

*'No, you won't. You'll go home and forget all about it.'*
*'I won't, I promise.'*
*'But what if you don't make it home? What if you get knocked down and killed as you cross the road to get the bus? What if the bus crashes and you're burnt to death? This graveyard is full of people who were going to do it when they got home. You have to do it now while the opportunity is here.'*
*'Ummm. OK. What do I have to do?'*
*'Just kneel down here with me and pray to God to forgive your sins and ask Jesus to come into your life.'*
*'Kneel? Here? In the middle of a graveyard.'*
*'Yeh. Cool, eh?'*

I always feel a bit bad about that one. But I did mean well. Honest.

*'Mez?'*
*'Yeh.'*
*'I need to talk to you.'*
*'But it's two o'clock in the morning!'*
*'I know, but I want you to pray with me. I need to give my life to God. I need to put my trust in Jesus.'*
*'OK. Where are you sleeping tonight?'*
*'At the Sally Army Hostel in town.'*
*'I'll be right over.'*

*'You're supposed to be one of those born again types, aren't you?'*
*'Yeh.'*
*'Well, tell me about this Jesus then. What's he ever done for me?'*
*'He died for your sins. How about that for starters?'*
*'Mez, I want to believe but my life is just so hard at the minute.'*
*'It'll be harder when you're spending eternity in hell.'*

That last technique isn't found in too many books on modern evangelism.

*I can talk to all these people about Jesus, but I don't really know much more than the basics. I think I want to go to Bible College. I'll get to hang out with loads of Christians and we'll talk about the Bible and pray and stuff, and all my questions will be answered. It will be absolute quality!*

# 12

# DIFFERENT FROM THE BROCHURE

*T*he room has two metal-framed beds, green prison issue blankets, whitewashed stone walls, a table and a sink in the corner. It smells musty and everything about it screams 'prison'. I feel my chest start to tighten. I can't stay here. I thought this was supposed to be a Bible college? This looks like a cell in Armley Jail.

'It'll be alright, Mez.'

I look at my friend and shake my head. There's no way I'm staying here. They'd practically dragged me kicking and screaming to a cell in prison so there was no way I was going to stay here voluntarily and pay for the privilege at the same time!

'It'll look much better with a few of your things and some pictures on the wall. Give it a go.'

I smile weakly and sit down heavily on the bed.

I wave them goodbye and head back to my cell, sorry, room. It didn't look like this on the brochure, but I suppose nothing ever does.

OK, a quick scan of the place to get my bearings. Kitchen, dining room, chapel area, sitting room, lecture rooms and library. Man, look at all these books about God and stuff! How mad is that? Maybe this place isn't going to be so bad after all.

*'How are you doing, Brother?'*

   *'What? Oh, OK.'*

   *'Praise the Lord! Praise his magnificent Name!'*

   *'Whatever, Mate.'*

   *My 'freakometer' is going into overdrive.*

*'Good evening everyone. Let me be the first to welcome you all to the College on behalf of the Student Union. I understand that some of you may be nervous about meeting new people, so let's try and break the ice, shall we? Turn to the person next to you, introduce yourself in a sentence and then give him a big hug in the Name of the Lord.'*

   *This guy has got to be joking. Hug them in the Name of the Lord! What's that supposed to mean?*

   *'Hi, my name's Pete and I'm from Essex.'*

   *'Well, good for you, Pete. I'm Mez, and don't even think about hugging me. Alright?'*

*How weird are this lot? There was a guy in the lounge playing a guitar and singing some cheesy songs about Jesus. People loved it. They were clapping and singing. One guy was even dancing! The guy was actually dancing! That can't be normal, can it?*

*I met a normal person today. His name is Steve and he's from Yorkshire, which goes a long way to explaining why he's about the only other sane bloke in this mad-house. To be fair, there are a few others but they appear to be few and far between.*

*College is nothing like I thought it would be. I thought it would be like church except I could ask loads of questions about my faith and people would take the time to sit down and answer them with me. But people are so introverted here. They just want to talk about their feelings all the time. I'm not interested in how I feel about my father and all that psycho-babble; I just want to know more about God, Jesus and the Bible. Apparently, that's not possible unless I 'understand myself'. Well, I think I understand myself pretty well. I was a liar, manipulator, thief, fornicator and all round scumbag. For some reason Jesus chose to die for me, and that will do for me. I can't pretend to understand it all, but I accept it gratefully. So, I'm just not interested in revisiting the past. I can't do anything about it, but with*

Jesus I can do something about the future. That's about the only 'self understanding' that I need.

Sometimes I just want to beat the living daylights out of some of these people. I seem to spend most of my time repenting at the moment. I'm supposed to love my brothers and sisters, am I not? I've been looking in the Bible to see if God makes exceptions in the case of idiots, but, sadly, I haven't found anything yet.

What are you doing here? You don't belong here. This is a place for proper Christians not wannabees like you. Come on, Mez, get real and disappear. Am I even really a Christian or am I just pretending? God, please take these thoughts out of my head. Help me to try and at least like some of these people.

I don't think I want to be a Christian anymore. It's too much like hard work trying to love people all the time when all I really want to do is smash their faces in. I suppose I'm not really used to the concept of debate. Where I come from the guy who wins the fight wins the debate.

Sometimes I wake up in my room and feel the presence of evil. I can't explain it, but it is so tangible that I can almost touch it.

### 'What, me?'

I've been given an assignment by the College. Apparently I've got to go with another guy and lead a Sunday morning service. I've never done anything like that before. All I've ever done is share my testimony, and that was hard enough. How am I supposed to lead a service?

Apparently I'm leading the 'worship' and prayer at the beginning of the service. I haven't a clue about worship and prayer. Most of the prayers I've heard people doing up the front go on for about fifteen minutes. How am I going to pray for fifteen minutes? What am I supposed to say? What about songs? I don't know any songs or hymns or stuff. I know. I'll just pick all the oldest hymns in the book. They're bound to know all the old ones.

## Scene: a packed church of 200 people in the South of England
## Occasion: my first ever service

'Well, morning everyone. How's it going?'

Silence.

'I said, how's it going?'

Silence.

'Oh well, let's knock out a hymn then, eh? Brush off the old cobwebs. I picked this one because it was written in the 1700s, so I'm hoping that most of you know it. Most of you look like you were around when it was originally written.'

Deafening silence.

'Right, let's get on our feet then and give it some welly.'

Some old geezer starts cracking out a tune on the organ. But it soon becomes apparent to me that nobody is singing this hymn. Not one person! In fact, the whole congregation is standing and staring dumbly at me.

'Hands up if you know this one. Nobody?'

Now what am I supposed to do? They didn't tell me how to handle this at college.

'Ah well, let's just sit down and have a quick prayer shall we?'

I stumble through the prayer and, as I end, I realise that I still have other obscure hymns up my sleeve.

'Listen folks, why don't you shout out a favourite hymn or song and we'll just bin the ones I've chosen, eh? OK? Nice one.'

Well you messed that up good and proper, didn't you? What do you think you're doing with these churchy types? You're an embarrassment. Just give it up and go home. Christian leader! What a joke!

'Are you Mez?'

'Yeh.'

'My name's Pete, and we've been assigned to visit a prison this term.'

'You're joking, aren't you? I'm not going to no prison!'

'You've got to.'

*'I don't have to do anything, Mate. Besides they'll never let me in a prison with my record.'*

*'They will. It's already been cleared, apparently.'*

*'Great! What muppet dreamt that up?'*

*'It'll be good. With your experience you'll be able to speak to their hearts.'*

*'Their hearts! What does that mean? Have you ever been to a prison?'*

*'No.'*

*'Well if you're coming with me, don't be saying freaky stuff like that. We'll be lucky to get out without being abused. Speak to their hearts! Are you people living in the twilight zone, or what?'*

## Scene: a prison chapel in the South of England
## Occasion: my first visit to a prison since my conversion

*'Hello gentlemen. My name is Pete and I used to be a policeman.'*
   *Somebody please help me!*

*I've started having flashbacks. There's no warning. When it happens it happens. Yesterday it happened while I was having dinner. All of a sudden I just lost it and started hallucinating. All the old feelings and fears just came flooding back. Sometimes it lasts for ten minutes and sometimes it lasts for a couple of hours. I seem to lose all control of my senses. I just repeat Psalm 23 to myself again and again and that seems to help.*

*I caught a guy praying in the toilets today and sprinkling some water or oil around. When I asked him what he was doing, he said he was 'cleansing' it from demons and evil spirits. Apparently the devil and his crew just hang around in toilets waiting to hassle people!*

*We had a lecture today on the creation of the world and everything kicked off! It was quality. People were getting well excited. The lecturer doesn't believe that God created the world in six days. He says it's far more intellectually acceptable for him to believe that God used evolution in order to fulfil his creative process. I've never thought about it before today but some people really went off the* deep end and were calling him a heretic. I don't know what a heretic is, but I bet it's the closest any of this lot ever come to using swear words! The lecturer said that we shouldn't put constraints on God and that he was quite capable of using evolution if he wanted to. It seemed pretty ironic that he was willing to accept that God could have created the world in millions of years yet completely dismiss the idea that he could have done it as simply stated in the Bible. I wondered who was doing the actual constraining.

## Labelled!

I found out today that I'm 'Reformed'. Apparently I have a choice between being this and 'charismatic'. I have absolutely no idea what they're talking about, but I've been put in the 'Reformed' camp anyway. One of my lecturers told me that I 'take the Bible too seriously and ought to make more effort to discover the experiential side of my faith'. I told him I would follow his advice if we opened the Bible in his class once in a while! Sometimes I get the feeling that some of these people are only a few pages ahead of us in the textbook.

'What you need, Mez, is the power of the Holy Spirit in your life.'
    'Is that right?'
    'Yes, your problem is that your faith is all intellectual and you've never had a real and powerful experience of the Holy Spirit.'
    'Is that right?'
    'Yes you need the power, Mez.'
    'The power? What power?'
    'The power to defeat sin, to rise up in the Name of the Holy Spirit and to witness to the glory of the gospel.'
    'Tell you what, muppet, why don't you and I take a walk around my old estate and we'll see where your power is. You wouldn't last two minutes in the real world.'

I had to share my testimony at a meeting tonight. People seem to like hearing my testimony but it always makes me feel uncomfortable. Many of these people seem so bored with their own testimonies that they need to hear mine. But I'm no more saved than they are. We all still get to go to the good place. A couple came to me afterwards *to tell me how wonderful I was. Wonderful! Yeh, I'm so wonderful that when I was younger I waited until one of my mates was away on holiday and then burgled his house. What a lovely young man I am! What a credit to my family!*

*One of my friends from the streets died today. He was found in a car park. He had ODed on smack and then choked to death on his own vomit. I didn't feel much like discussing whether signs and wonders were a legitimate tool for evangelism in the modern world.*

## Scene: a church soup kitchen in Bournemouth, England
## Occasion: the Holy Spirit prompts me to pray

He must have been in his late forties. There was nothing outstanding about him. We'd had a hundred plus men in during the morning, but for some reason I was drawn to him. I tried to talk to him but he just wanted his soup and that was it. So I sat and watched him from behind the counter. And then from nowhere I felt this urge to pray for him. It just rose up within me and I felt that I would explode if I didn't pray for him there and then. I tried to fight the feeling and wondered if I was having a panic attack. I even went into another room but I couldn't find any peace. Pray for him, the voice kept telling me over and over again. I had been helping out for months and nothing like this had ever happened to me before. It wasn't like I even knew this guy very well. As I didn't know what I was supposed to pray, I just prayed that God would have mercy on him and save his soul. But the Holy Spirit wouldn't let me stop there so I just continued to pray for him, really pray for him. I discovered his name from one of the other men and found a tract to give him to read, but he had gone by the time I had sorted myself out. Two days later he was dead. Found in a grotty hostel, alone in the world. Lost for eternity, for all I knew.

Sometimes some of the students roll in drunk from night clubs and I wonder what I'm doing here. Then they're up in chapel the next day singing songs and praising God like nothing's ever happened. Apparently, they feel the need to go to these clubs to show people how 'cool' Christians are. Funny how these 'cool' types are often the biggest freaks of the lot. They should leave well alone, if you ask me. I hear more stories of believers getting drunk than of people being saved.

*I'm going back home today. I've made it to the end of my first year and I haven't killed anybody. I can't wait to get out of here and see my mates.*

**Scene: Bible College - Year Two**
**Occasion: class on spiritual renewal**

*'So, as we can see, demonisation can seriously affect the Christian believer.'*

*'Are you saying Christians can be possessed by the devil?'*

*'Yes, I suppose I am. But they are more likely to be Christians who have come from difficult backgrounds. In fact, these are the signs to watch out for: broken home, drug addiction, prison and occultism.'*

*'You're talking rubbish, Mate. Where's our assurance if we can be possessed by the devil any time he wants?'*

*I am dismissed. Apparently I have the demon of unbelief.*

*'I've a new tutor this year and he's sound as a pound. He's never too busy to see me and he never makes me feel like I'm intruding on him. I can just jabber away to him and he's sympathetic to my fears and problems especially with the more charismatic elements in the college.*

*I've made a couple of good friends here. One in particular, Chris, is just a normal, down-to-earth bloke. We often chat and pray together. He makes me feel that you don't have to be a complete fruit bat in order to be a Christian.*

*Doctrine, Hermeneutics and Exegesis. I didn't have a clue what they even meant a year ago but now I'm completely fascinated by them. I hope this doesn't mean I'm turning into some sad Christiany type.*

*The Bible is just an amazing book, complex yet simple at the same time.*

*Anthropomorphisms, ethnocentricity, ethnomusicology, contextualisation, blah, blah, blah. What was that all about? I can honestly say that I didn't understand a single word of the lesson. I feel like a right muppet, particularly when everyone is going 'mmm' after everything that our lecturer said. At least the lecturer is amusing. He's a real ringer for that little green fella in Star Wars. It's been doing my head in all lesson trying to think of his name. Yoda! That's his name. I'm being taught by Yoda!*

*I'm glad that my faith doesn't rest on how I feel. Most of the time I don't feel particularly great at all, but I know that at any time I can turn to God in his Word and he'll be there. He's my Constant, the anchor in my life when I'm feeling adrift. I'm not one for all this emotional stuff, but I know deep down, in my own way, I love God and I love his Word. His love for me will never change. That's much more certain than my fragile emotional state.*

*If I've learned one thing this year it's that the Bible stands above all our spiritual experiences and us. It's the final arbiter in all things. It's flawless and completely trustworthy on all things. The more I understand and trust the Bible the stronger I feel my faith becomes. I don't feel so antagonistic toward people these days. I don't much like them, but at least I'm willing to talk to them - even those I consider to be muppets. It's an improvement, I suppose.*

*I've got to learn to love these people. God loves me and all my (many) faults. Still, I find it so hard. Sometimes I wake up at night and pray that God will just take my anger from me. But then the next day somebody annoys me and I have to start again.*

*Bible College is not the place I thought it was going to be. It's just full of ordinary Joe's (and some not so ordinary!) - sinful, fallen people just like me. I just wish that some of them weren't so freaky at the same time!*

*I got my degree tonight. Had the hat and gown and the full works. I was well chuffed. Me with a degree! Bring on the world.*

# WHITE SOCKS AND SANDALS

I can't remember exactly when I saw a real live missionary for the first time. I'm almost sure that it was at a midweek meeting in my home church in Swindon. It was almost certainly during my first few months at Bible College.

I don't remember names or even places. It was a family of four though: mum, dad, son and daughter. My only real abiding memory was of the sandals with accompanying white socks, and the brown trousers resting slightly below the ankle but high enough to have a comical effect. Then there was the mum in her large print dress and their two children trying desperately to look like they really wanted to be up in front singing some sort of tribal song with their mum and dad. It played like a scene from the twilight zone.

I didn't think I would make a very good missionary. The most cross-cultural experience I'd ever had was putting curry sauce on my chips. Missionaries all seemed to play a musical instrument and wear freakish clothes. I was so glad that I was going to be sticking in this county.

I remember my first 'missiology' lecture at college. I remember thinking, 'Missiology? What's that when it's at home?' Turns out that it was the study of missions. Why don't these people just call it that then? They seemed to have an 'ology' for everything at Bible College.

*I read an amazing book today called 'Bruchko'. It's about a guy God used to work with Indians in South America. Just incredible!*

*I read another book today by a guy called Richard Wurmbrand. Why aren't we ready to die for our faith?*

*I read a book today about a Christian drug rehabilitation centre in Northern Spain. Inspirational.*

*We used to have people from missionary societies visit us every week at Bible College. Every Friday afternoon it was. For a lot of students it was just a time to catch up on sleep or pop off into town to get something decent to eat. I remember one month very vividly.*

## Week One

*Friday morning - last lecture before dinner. It's always a killer lecture because it's the last one before we break up for the weekend. I feel sorry for these poor spuds that have to come and do it. Nobody's really listening, but these guys come in week after week and speak about their particular mission. Last week a guy came and told us about his 'ministry' and how he cut people's gardens in order to win an opportunity to share the gospel with them. I haven't a clue who we've got this week. I haven't bothered checking the board.*

*'Good morning. Today I would like to share with you about our work with the street children of Cambodia.'*

*Street children? Did he say street children? Why does that sound familiar to me? It's ringing a bell for some reason, but I can't remember why.*

*'Street children constitute the largest unreached people group in the world today. They are often the weakest, most vulnerable and despised members of their communities, and little or nothing is being done to alleviate the problem by the modern church.'*

*How sad is that? The church ought to pull itself together on this one.*

'If anybody would like to know more about our work then pick up a leaflet afterwards and get in contact with us. We would love to hear from you.'

*I've been lying awake for hours thinking about those street children. Somebody really ought to do something about it.*

## Week two

*We've got a bloke from some Romanian mission coming in today. Maybe I'll just squeeze myself in at the back and get on with some reading while he's blabbering on.*

'These pictures were taken last week in a government controlled children's home.'

*Pale, wide-eyed, panic stricken, hungry, malnourished, unloved, unwashed, completely broken by life. I could not take my eyes off the photos or the legions of children they showed. They all looked utterly alone.*

*This just is not right. I'm getting mad now. Why doesn't somebody do something about it? We're all sitting here eating dinner and laughing and joking like we'd never seen those photos. How can we do this? How can we just pretend it's not happening?*

## Week Three

'Hello, I am with Latin Link. Did you know that there are more children living on the streets of Brazil than in any other country in the world today?'

*I can't sleep. I can't eat. I keep dreaming of street children reaching out to touch me, to grab me, begging me to help them. What can I do? I'm not a missionary. I'm not the type. I'm staying in England and working here. But somebody ought to do something about those street children. It's an absolute crime.*

*Maybe I ought to do something about those street children.*

*I can't be going to Brazil. I don't even like flying. The thought of getting on an aeroplane makes me feel sick.*

'Dear Lord, if you want me to go to Brazil and work with street children then send me a clear sign or something.'

*I got a book in the post today. Sent anonymously. It's a book about the street children of Brazil. Somebody is playing with my head. It took me about three hours to read it.*

*'I need a clearer sign, Lord. Brazil is a long way away.'*

### Week Four

*'Who's doing the mission spot this week?'*

*'Dunno. Some chap from UFM Worldwide.' (Unevangelised Fields Mission Worldwide)*

*'What do they do?'*

*'I'm not sure.'*

*'I hope it's nothing to do with street children. We've had that guilt trip for three weeks in a row now.'*

*'Hello. My name is Keith Cornell and I would like to talk to you today about some of the ministry opportunities with UFMW.'*

*That's a relief. This guy has been talking for twenty minutes and not even a hint of a street child.*

*'Well, thanks for listening so well. Just before I take questions, let me just end by telling you a little about a street children project we are involved with in a place called Belém at the mouth of the Amazon River.'*

*'Excuse me, Mr Cornell?'*

*'Can I help you?'*

*'Well, I think God might be talking to me, sort of, if that doesn't sound too weird, about going to Brazil and doing some street children stuff. Do you know what I mean? The problem is that I'm not sure if it's him or me talking, and even if it isn't me, I'm not sure that this is my sort of gig. I know I'm supposed to say that God's speaking to my heart but I haven't really got a clue what that means. But I do think that I should be doing something about this street kids' thing. What do you reckon?'*

*'Young man, I have no clue what you have just said to me, but why don't you take a form, go away and pray about it and then, if you still feel God's leading in your life, fill it in and send it off.'*

'Alright. Nice one.'
'My pleasure.'

'OK, Lord, here's the deal. I'm going to send this form off to UFMW now and if it doesn't come back within a week then I'll take that as a clear and final answer to all the street children stuff.'

Three days later

*I got a letter from UFMW this morning from some guy named George. He sounds pretty cool. He wants me to get in touch with him so that we can talk about the 'Lord's calling'. The Lord's calling - I'm not sure what that means, but I'm almost positive that I should be going to Brazil to work with street children.*

# 14

# THE END ... OR NOT

A ll stories must come to an end. It's the other unbreakable rule of storytelling, I suppose. But even as I draw my tale to a close it's not really the end of the story. In some respects it's just the beginning.

I married Miriam at the beginning of August 1998, and two months later we visited UFMW's street children project in the city of Belém at the mouth of the Amazon River. We spent two months there and had what I would describe as a mixed experience. The mission field, like college before it, was nothing like my naïve, utopian dreams. However, we returned home more convinced than ever that it was where we wanted to serve God. We didn't know it then, but we would have to wait another five years before we finally made it on to the mission field.

After leaving Bible College in 1999 I took a job as an associate pastor in a Baptist church. Once again my dreams were shattered by the reality of life in church leadership. I was a young man and inexperienced in the ministry. It was a somewhat turbulent time and I resigned after less than a year in the post. That affected Miriam and me very deeply. Our faith in people, especially Christians, was shattered. Those who had once called themselves friends turned against us, but we felt the decision to leave was right at the time. Our faith in the church was likewise damaged, and it would be more than six months before I could stomach sitting in a church building again. It was not all bad, and we left with friendships that continue to this day. As I look back on that period I can certainly see God's grace at work, and events in later ministries have shown me that I gained valuable lessons and insights from my short time with that community.

We then moved to Birmingham where I worked with a good and honest man from whom I learned a lot. In my two years there we faced pastoral difficulties and personal crises far more serious than in my previous ministry. Yet, despite its faults and mine, it was a community in which we felt loved and supported under the leadership of godly, sincere men of integrity, committed to God and the gospel of the Lord Jesus Christ.

## Passports please

*Miriam and I arrived in Brazil in September 2003 with our two young daughters. Keziah was about eighteen months old and Lydia was a year younger. We turned up with eleven suitcases and not a clue about what we were actually going to be doing there. In the three years that we've been here, we've had to leave the field twice due to illness. Both our girls have been in hospital on more than one occasion and we've found the whole missionary experience very wearing. Why are we here? That's a question that often surfaces, and it was one that was particularly hard to answer as we watched our eight-month-old daughter strapped to a bed with tubes sticking out of her. We couldn't even ask the doctor for help or clarification because we didn't have a common language.*

We have wanted to leave so many times that we've lost count. It's been a struggle spiritually, physically and emotionally. We've felt depressed and often quite isolated. Those emotions worsen when we hear of friends being married, or family members having children, and we're not there to share in their special moments.

Sometimes we worry that our children will be the strange cousins that nobody really knows. Then there is their education. There is so much to make us wonder if we're doing the right thing.

And yet I'm thankful to God for my life. I'm thankful to God for my wife. She's a constant source of strength and encouragement. I'm thankful for my girls. They are precious gifts from God. As I'm typing these words my youngest, Lydia, has just toddled into my office. Keziah is singing that the best book to read is the Bible.

I look at my wife, my girls, my life and I see the power of the gospel. The true power, not just the intellectual proposition that says unless you repent and believe you will perish for all eternity. The glorious gospel of the Lord Jesus Christ is so much bigger than anything we could ever imagine.

The greatest sermon that I ever heard was in a prison visiting room when two men walked in, looked me straight in the eyes and said, 'How are you, Mez?' If I'm honest, that was the moment when I realised the gospel was true. Hell held no fear for me at that time. I needed hope; I needed the promise of, not only peace with God, but also peace of mind. I needed a reason to go on, a reason to exist. And I needed to connect with the human race once again.

Jesus Christ has not only freed me from my sin, he has not only reconciled me to God, but he has changed my future and the future of my offspring for generations to come. He has broken the chains that bound me from birth. The cycle of pain and misery will stop with me. My children will never know what it is to be beaten at home. They will never know what it is to be abused physically and mentally by those who are meant to care for them. God willing, they will never know what it is like to go hungry. They will never know all these things because of the transforming power of the gospel of Jesus Christ in **my** life. Jesus Christ has broken the cycle. I can't protect them from the world around them, and I can't protect them from their own sinful inclinations, but I can offer them an environment in which the gospel is real and relevant to their lives.

I can offer them hope, opportunities and dreams. I can offer them things they could never have imagined if God had not reached down from heaven and given me life.

We all grow up at some point. I'd like to say that I've held on to my early naivety, but I haven't. I have, in a way, adopted everything that I first found strange about the Christian culture and lifestyle. I don't know how it happened. It just sort of snuck up on me, I suppose.

Jesus was right when he said that the cost would be high if we follow him. I've seen many friends fall by the wayside in the years since Bible College. I've seen many people start on the Christian road only to stumble and disappear from sight. But I've clung to the cross, sometimes by my fingernails, and God has helped me to persevere through difficult times.

I want to say that I've forgiven everybody in my life, but I'm not sure if that would be honest. However, I'm no longer consumed by hate. I'm consumed by serving my Lord and Saviour. I'm consumed with Jesus Christ. I don't skip down the road every morning whistling a tune whilst the birds sing in the trees because that's not real life. But I will not let the past dominate my life and influence my future any more. The Bible says that 'the old has gone' and it truly has. I'm not a recovering drug addict; I'm not a recovering anything. I'm a new creation and all because of the power of God.

Although I've felt a strange mixture of emotions in writing this book, my overall feeling has been one of deep gratitude to God for the love, compassion and grace he has shown me in the death and resurrection of Jesus Christ. What seemed like a fairy story when I was a boy, and a complete irrelevance to me in my teenage years has, ironically, turned out to be my salvation.

This book has been six years in the writing. I've stopped and started it many times, mainly because I was unsure of my real motivation. I don't think that there is one definitive reason why I've written it. But one reason is that I wanted to try and make sense of those early years, to try and put my teens and early twenties into some kind of perspective. If I'm honest, I only realised through writing it how I felt then. Have I written everything that could be said or described, every emotion that I experienced? Of course not. Time and fading memories make that impossible.

The contrast between the person I was before Christ, and the person I am today because of Christ, is so enormous that I sometimes find it difficult to believe all that has happened. The transition from one life to the other has been hugely difficult for me. Many people handed me 'testimony' books in the early days, books full of stories of those who had been rescued by God. I found no solace in them. They were amazing stories that offered me no insights as to how to cope 'post conversion'. They all seemed to end happily ever after, whereas I seemed to lurch from one crisis to another. Satan really played with my mind and sometimes I wondered if I was going mad.

Ironically, salvation from my battles within lay in the very place that I found most confusing and alien; it lay in the church. I found the church to be a place of surprising contradictions. There were those, for whatever reason, who would have liked to see me fall and fail, but there have been many who have picked me up, encouraged me in the faith and helped me to keep on going. There have been great men and women of God who knew absolutely nothing about my life experience yet who were my greatest helps because of their Christ-like, godly lives.

The church is the key to surviving troubled times. For all its faults, God has given us the church with its pains and troubles as a place in which we can grow and mature. I think back and shudder at some of my early attitudes and behaviour. Yet I also think back and thank God for those who stuck with me in my darkest times, who didn't give up on me even when I was giving up on myself.

I don't know what surprises, what heartaches, what moments of happiness life has in store for me and my family. But I do know that it is all in the hands of God Almighty and that somehow it is all wrapped up within the immense cosmic story that was written in eternity past and will continue into eternity future. And I know one last thing: whatever happens in this life or the next one, I will never, for one moment, be alone again.

# 15

# SAVED TO SERVE

God did a wonderful thing when he saved my soul, but what amazes me beyond words is that he redeemed my circumstances too. All those years when I was beaten, hurt, alone, and desperate – he has even redeemed them. They are the tools that help me to understand the children we meet day by day on the streets. When I look into their dead eyes and suspicious faces I know what lurks behind them. That's why this book finishes, not with the end of the story of my life, but with the beginning of the story of our work here in Brazil.

I often think back to my time in Lindholme Prison. I would spend hours just walking around the perimeter fence looking out at the houses and people beyond. I wondered about their lives and their families: their hopes and dreams. I tried to imagine what my life would be like ten years into the future. Would I have a wife? Children? A house? A car? A good job? All the things that supposedly constitute a happy and fulfilled life.

Ten years later I am writing this at my desk in hot and humid Sao Luis, in northern Brazil. I am writing from a place that never even entered my mind in those days. And I am writing as a missionary involved with a project that I never even dreamed about. My life couldn't be further from what I imagined it to be on those cold, lonely walks around the prison yard. Such is the power of the gospel.

I have agonised and battled over how best to finish this book, how to describe the work we are involved with out here in Sao Luis. Miriam and I are now the directors of a project called, **Off The Streets**. Such is the scope of this project that I am finding it difficult to put it into words.

I suppose I could write about our drop-in centre that operates three mornings a week, our proposed recuperation home for addicts, our night work on the streets of the city, our pre-school for children from impoverished and broken homes, our crèche, football school, our alternative church for street children, alcoholics, lesbians and drug addicts. I could write about our vision statement and objectives to reach out to street children, children at risk and their families in the city. I could also write about our emphasis on prevention in the war against the street child problem. And I could write about our emergency shelter for children under twelve years old that we are in the process of building. I could write about our dream of creating a haven for used and abused children and young people in Sao Luis. Or I could just simply write about the people.

Thallison is twelve years old and we found him living under a bridge in one of the tourist hotspots in the city. He stole some money from his mum and hadn't returned home for six months when we found him. Thallison was living with a gang of about eight other children and a couple of adults, who were abusing him sexually. The boy was often paid for sex by visiting German and Dutch businessmen. When we discovered him he was emaciated, starving and high on paint thinner. Over a period of a few months our night team got to know him better and he slowly began to trust us. Eventually, we traced his family and found that his mum and grandma had been frantically searching for him for months. They were desperately worried and had long forgiven him for stealing from them. Emotions were running high as we took him back to be reunited with his family. All his family were there: mum, grandma, sister, brother and cousins. There were tears and hugs as he was welcomed back. Our team bought a little cake and spent a good hour praising and thanking God for this reunion.

When Thallison applied to return to school he was rejected because he didn't have a uniform, shoes or school books. **Off The Streets** agreed to vouch for him, bought his books and material, a uniform and his first ever pair of school shoes. Thallison is now back in school and dreams of becoming a doctor. He is the only member of his household who goes to church every Sunday to hear the Word of God and he is constantly sharing his new found faith with them. For the first time in a long time he has hopes and dreams for his future. Such is the power of the gospel and the grace of God.

George was thirteen years old when we found him living under the same bridge selling his body to passing tourists. He now lives at home with his aunty and is involved with a project that helps street children return back into full time education.

Innocencia is in her early twenties and has lived on the streets for over fifteen years. She walks with a pronounced limp because one of her feet is severely twisted after she was run over by a bus. Staff at the public hospital refused to treat her because she was a street child and her injury has never been treated properly. After two years of weekly contact through our drop-in centre work she has begun attending church services on Sunday mornings. She recently confessed Christ as her Saviour and she now works voluntarily as a cleaner at our community centre. Innocencia is posing some difficult questions for our work out here. We feel her confession of faith is genuine and yet we have been unable to find suitable living accommodation for her in order to help her move on with her life. Currently we are in the process of trying to rehouse her and seek help with her solvent abuse problem.

Romilson is eighteen years old and has lived on the streets for fifteen years. His father is a convicted rapist and he doesn't know his mother. Romilson has been coming along to our project off and on for about two years. He is violent and aggressive and regularly threatens our volunteers and staff. The young man suffers from severe mental problems due to prolonged substance abuse. He has not responded to the gospel and continually causes problems for us both inside ad outside of our centre. We continue to pray for him.

Kosmo, aged four, and Thais, aged six, are a brother and sister who began attending our inaugural pre-school at the community centre/church in J.Lima, one of the poorest neighbourhoods in the city and one that has huge economic and social problems. They have no mother and their father is a chronic alcoholic. They used to live in a run down shack with no front door, toilet or running water. Thais weighed less than a three year old when she came to us. Between 2pm and 5pm every weekday they had the opportunity to come to our school to help give them an educational leg up for when they start school officially at six years old. They often arrived hungry and dirty and sometimes their father was so drunk he forgot to come and get them. Recently they were evicted from their shack near our centre and we have not heard from them since. We continue to pray.

For every success story we have two more heartbreakers. Ours is not an easy job but it is an immense privilege to be here sharing the good news of Jesus Christ. In fact, it is the best job in the world. There are times, of course, when emotions run high and thoughts of quitting enter our minds. Wise friends, good churches and a supportive Mission have helped us through many such times.

I remember looking out of my window at night as a boy and wondering about the world, wondering about my future. I remember that, in spite of my circumstances, I cherished the secret dream that there was something better out there for me. And I hid those dreams deep inside so that SHE couldn't get them and squash them. Sometimes, in the dark moments, I would forget them for a while. But usually they resurfaced, a little spring of hope in a world of pain.

**Off The Streets** is primarily about the gospel of the Lord Jesus Christ. As poor as these people are, they are sinners cut off from God, and their only chance of redemption is faith in the finished work of Jesus Christ. But it is also about restoring dreams to suffering children. It is about giving them hope and the opportunity to realise that the world extends beyond their current circumstances and that they can play a constructive part in it. **Off The Streets** is about showing them and telling them that there is somebody 'out there' who cares for them and loves them. Years ago a missionary once said to me, 'Why are you always talking to these kids about hopes and dreams? They need to live in reality'.

On the contrary, their lives can be changed forever by the one true hope of the world – Jesus Christ – and any of their dreams can become a reality. Just ask a forgotten, neglected, angry, self destructive little boy who grew up on a rough council estate, having his dreams sucked out of him by the harshness of life and the cynicism of his elders. One day he grew up to become a missionary amongst street children, and his dreams were not only realised but they surpassed even his vivid imagination. That is the true power of the gospel of Jesus Christ and the complete, unmerited grace of God, our heavenly Father.

# Christian Focus Publications

publishes books for all ages

**STAYING FAITHFUL**

In dependence upon God we seek to help make His infallible Word, the Bible, relevant. Our aim is to ensure that the Lord Jesus Christ is presented as the only hope to obtain forgiveness of sin, live a useful life and look forward to heaven with Him.

**REACHING OUT**

Christ's last command requires us to reach out to our world with His gospel. We seek to help fulfill that by publishing books that point people towards Jesus and help them develop a Christ-like maturity. We aim to equip all levels of readers for life, work, ministry and mission.

Books in our adult range are published in three imprints.

*CHRISTIAN FOCUS* contains popular works including biographies, commentaries, basic doctrine and Christian living. Our children's books are also published in this imprint.

*MENTOR* focuses on books written at a level suitable for Bible College and seminary students, pastors, and other serious readers. The imprint includes commentaries, doctrinal studies, examination of current issues and church history.

*CHRISTIAN HERITAGE* contains classic writings from the past.

Christian Focus Publications, Ltd
Geanies House, Fearn, Ross-shire,
IV20 1TW, Scotland, United Kingdom
info@christianfocus.com

For details of our titles visit us on our website

www.christianfocus.com